LOST TRIBE

THE PEOPLE'S MEMORIES

BACK HOME IN EVERTON & SCOTTIE ROAD

TrinityMirror Media

by Ken Rogers

TrinityMirror Media

LOST TRIBE – THE PEOPLE'S MEMORIES
By Ken Rogers

Design & Production: Vicky Andrews, Zoë Bevan, Adam Oldfield

Produced by Trinity Mirror Media
Executive Editor: Ken Rogers
Senior Editor: Steve Hanrahan
Editor: Paul Dove
Senior Art Editor: Rick Cooke
Trinity Mirror Media Marketing Executive: Claire Brown
Sales and Marketing Manager: Elizabeth Morgan
Book Sales Executive: Karen Cadman
Liverpool Post & Echo Image Archive: Brian Johnston

Photographic credits:
Liverpool Daily Post & Echo
Trinity Mirror North West & North Wales
The Liverpool Records Office
The Shrewsbury House Archive Team
Lee Jones Collection
Mirrorpix
Billy Ellis

Cover image: The houses might have been feeling the passage of time, but cleanliness was next to godliness
in inner city areas like Everton. These ladies in China Street always ensured their front steps were scrubbed clean.

ISBN: 9781 9068 02998

Printed and bound by CPI Group (UK) Ltd, Croydon, CR0 4YY

ACKNOWLEDGEMENTS

Bibliography:
Liverpool Post & Echo
Liverpool Stage – *by Harold Ackroyd*
Vanished Liverpool and the San'tree Man – *by Brian Read*
Liverpool Heroes (Book 1), the stories of 16 Liverpool holders of the Victoria Cross
edited and researched by Ann Clayton, further research by Sid Lindsay and Bill Sergeant
Discover Liverpool – *by Ken Pye*
A History of the County of Lancaster: Volume 3 – *by William Farrer and*
J. Brownbill (1907)
Liverpool Under Charles 1 – *by George Chandler*

My thanks go to:
The Liverpool Records' Office
Kevin Roach *for his longstanding enthusiasm for the 'Lost Tribe' project*
Ken Pye *for his remarkable local history knowledge*
Rev. Kate Wharton *Vicar of St. George's Church, Everton*
Bob Harrington and John Simpson *the Parish Committee of St. George's Church*
Rev. Henry Corbett *Vicar of St. Peter's Church, Everton*
Councillor Jane Corbett *for her on-going community work for the people of Everton*
John Hutchison *and the Everton Park Heritage Trail working group*
The 'Friends of Everton Park' *for their love of a great district*
Ken and June Taylor *for their constant support with particular reference to my old
school Major Lester*
Joan Murray *for her stories and inspiration about the history of Everton*
Everton & District History Society *for inspiring interest in a remarkable area*
Tony McGann (OBE, MBE) *for having a different inner city vision*
George Evans (Chief Executive, Eldonians) *for his views on the 'clearances'*
Sam Perry *and the Shrewsbury House Archive team*
Friends of the Liverpool History Society – *Facebook platform*
Liverpool 5 (Everton, Vauxhall, Kirkdale) – *Facebook platform*
Margaret Bowden *for rescuing the swimming baths pictures*
Danny Mannion *for his Conway and Robsart Street images*
To all those contributors to my Liverpool Echo 'Lost Tribe' column
who have provided some remarkable personal stories for this book

To those near and far who continue to exchange memories on
www.losttribeofeverton.com

CONTENTS

CONTENTS

TRIBUTE IN VERSE TO THE FRIENDS AND NEIGHBOURS WHO WERE SCATTERED
FAR AND WIDE IN THE SIXTIES CLEARANCES, BUT WHO NOW RETURN EVERY
YEAR FOR THE 'LOST TRIBE STREET REUNIONS' WHERE WE PROUDLY
REMEMBER THE WAY IT WAS, WHILE REVELLING IN THE WAY IT IS . . .

—— ∞ ——

'LOST TRIBE' BACK ON SACRED GROUND

The journey home is now complete
The Lost Tribe – back in Everton's streets
In our mind's eye, our Nins, our Nans
Our Dads, old Pop, our dear old Grans

Grandad's medals shine again
Reminding us when men were men
Our mams still there to stir our souls
And help us all to reach our goals

The Council sent us far away
They called it our Slum Clearance Day
They built us flats ten storeys high
With 'streets' that floated in the sky

They said we wouldn't have it hard
But High Rise flats don't have a yard
And how are mams supposed to dream
Without a sandstone step to clean?

Why bother with an open door
When Mary's on another floor?
Or even in another town
Why did they knock our old streets down?

But now we've started coming home
To climb Mount Everton and roam
Atop that hill that's still a jewel
The greatest view in Liverpool

The Lost Tribe – back in Everton's streets
Sacred ground beneath our feet.

—— ∞ ——

CHECK OUT WWW.LOSTTRIBEOFEVERTON.COM
TO DISCOVER THE DATE OF THE NEXT
'LOST TRIBE' STREET REUNION

HOW THE LOST TRIBE FOUND ITS WAY HOME TO WALK ONCE MORE ON EVERTON'S STEEP SLOPES

Your letters, emails
and pictures
instinctively led to
this second book
— every word is
a tribute to your
incredible passion
for the old streets

THE first edition of 'Lost Tribe of Everton & Scottie Road' – written to mark the 50th anniversary of the Liverpool City Council's controversial 1960s slum clearance programme – captured the interest of a worldwide audience and the feedback was truly remarkable.

I've had letters and emails from all over the globe and it has been clear that the memory banks have been going into re-wind and then fast forward as if sparked and brought back to life by an old accumulator. If you don't know what the latter is, you might want to flick forward to Chapter 38, but I suggest you just go with the flow as this second 'Lost Tribe' journey unfolds to remind us once again of the way it used to be.

I hope that, with every turn of the page, you will be transported back to another time, another place, another planet – that remarkable era of the mid 1940s to the 1960s.

For me, it was a world full of terraced houses in steep streets, sweeping down in regimented straight lines from the summit of Mount Everton to the Dock Gates of the Mersey, criss-crossed every half mile or so by the wide and powerful horizontal lines of Netherfield Road, Great Homer Street, the mighty 'Scottie', and Vauxhall Road beyond. Any further takes you 'Over the Bridge' which is another story in its own right.

I shared many of my own personal family stories in the first 'Lost Tribe' book behind a heartfelt belief that you would see your street in my street, your grandparents in my grandparents, and your childhood in my childhood. However, I had no perception of the response I would get from fellow proud members of the 'Lost Tribe of Everton & Scottie Road' and other inner city dwellers. To say that it has been inspirational is an under-statement.

Your letters, emails and pictures instinctively led to this second book – *The People's Memories*. Every word is a tribute to your incredible passion for the old streets.

So let me set the scene once more as we climb back into our time machine with the dial set for any day in the 1950s. In our mind's eye, we are looking down once more on a seemingly never-ending panorama of slate roofs, smoking chimneys, tiny backyards, and narrow back entries

Our hearts miss a beat, but it's not inspired by a fleeting memory of a first girlfriend or boyfriend. It's actually much more romantic than that.

This is a love story inspired by the old districts themselves where we left our hearts, but retained our remarkable lifetime memories when the 'slum clearance' bulldozers came to call and destroyed a community marriage that had lasted for 150 years.

My aim in writing the first 'Lost Tribe' book was to ensure that the people and the families forced out of their spiritual home would have their own place in the social history of our city. In many respects, we had become the forgotten people of Liverpool and yet over 125,000 of us were directly affected by the Council's clearance exercise.

Our streets had soared up the spectacular 'Mount Everton' from base camp on the rough and tough Scotland Road, first traversing the remarkable shopping district of Great Homer Street and then the Orange and Green buffer areas of Netherfield Road North / South and Shaw Street before finally reaching the upper ridge line of St. Domingo Road / Heyworth Street and Everton Road.

We are talking about an area of less than one and a half square miles, but several hundred terraced streets were shoe-horned between the boundary lines, many of them amongst the most densely populated in the country.

Suddenly these streets were gone, buried under the greenery of the modern but disjointed Everton Park.

Who put the lights out? An old gas lamp looks forlorn on Queens Road

My first task was to write a book that would commit to public record the memories, trials, tribulations and achievements of the generations who had gone before.

In other words, the period from the pioneering days of the mid-1800s when our great grandparents combined with an army of Irish 'invaders' to claim the dock lowlands up to the emerging Scottie Road. This tribe then invaded the highlands of Upper Everton where the great and the good had built their mansions along a hilltop garden paradise that would now become a fully functional working class concrete jungle.

My second task was to build a website www.losttribeofeverton.com that would enable the scattered members of the 'Lost Tribe of Everton and Scottie Road' to communicate again, wherever they might be. The beauty of the internet is the interactive opportunities it throws up and I'm proud to say that thousands of people have been able to find each other and exchange personal memories about grandparents, parents and neighbours.

Friends who were cast to the four corners of Merseyside by the clearances have been able to catch up again, many of them making contact for the first time in half a century. That's an awful lot of catching up to do, but it's happening on the site every single day and the end product is a growing and valuable archive of street memories.

www.losttribeofeverton.com will remain 'live' for years to come. It provides a platform to record your own stories of street games, school days, the seasons, the Christmas memories of yesteryear, the war stories, the characters and the major events within a key phase in your life.

I also hope you use the website's 'Memory' and 'Street Search' buttons in a much more simplistic way.

Just go online and type in the name of your parents and grandparents, say how much they mean to you and – if they are no longer with us – say how much you miss them. Conjure up some simple images in your mind.

A metal tin bath hanging on a rusty nail on the wall of a tiny lime-washed backyard . . .

A cast iron mangle . . .

An outside lavatory with its candle as the only light source and with the Liverpool Echo, ripped into neat strips, hanging on a piece of string (the usual great read, but clearly a massively important multi-purpose product in those days) . . .

A tiny back kitchen with its functional gas stove bringing a pan of Scouse or barley soup to the boil . . .

A welcoming open fire burning in a hearth.

A cellar or attic, exciting and mysterious.

Your father telling his old war stories.

Your mother introducing you like a celebrity to complete strangers in shops or at bus stops: *This is my lovely son / daughter . . .'*

You cringe at the time, and back away embarrassed. But you remember these things later in life and realise that such open expressions of family pride are priceless.

If you are reading this, there is a very good chance you will be a fully paid-up member of the 'Lost Tribe of Everton & Scottie Road'.

If you are from any inner city area, you are also one of us.

But like I said in my first book, just by taking the trouble to read this title and find out about this period in our city's social history, you are guaranteed a very warm welcome through our ever-open front doors.

This book majors on the 'PEOPLE'S MEMORIES' and what incredible stories you have been sending me.

Over the past 12 months I have been collecting and collating your personal tales, publishing many of them in my weekly 'Lost Tribes' column in the Saturday edition of the Liverpool Echo newspaper. I assume the latter doesn't hang in your toilet these days!

Like most people who work in a modern office, I can feel swamped by the grind and monotony of dealing with hundreds of emails, many totally unnecessary. There's something very different about receiving a 'proper' letter or communication, something that feels special and personal.

I've opened every piece of your correspondence with all the excitement and expectation of being invited by an old neighbour for an impromptu chat and a cup of tea.

Your pride in the old streets, your parents, your grandparents, and the togetherness that we all took for granted is matched only by the unique humour of a community family who all have different surnames, but who are very much part of the same tribe, in our case the *Great Tribe of Everton & Scottie Road* who ultimately became my *'Lost Tribe'* after the 1960s slum clearance exercise.

In personally meeting thousands of people since the launch of my first book – be it at the hugely successful summer street reunions at St. George's Church in Everton, or at a variety of talks and discussions with community groups and local history groups across Merseyside – I've only had one person question the use of the word 'tribe' in the title. One lady sought me out to suggest it made the people sound like savages.

I was happy to have the debate because she couldn't be further from the truth.

The 'Original Roget's (not Rogers) Thesaurus of English Words and Phrases' gives the following alternatives for the word 'Tribe' – *family, race, group, breed, multitude, genealogy, native, community.*

As a boy from Netherfield Road North, I will happily sign up to all of those because I still feel that we were and are a special *family* from a *race* that sometimes begged to differ when it came to issues like the 'Orange and the Green', but fundamentally stood together as a *group* through two World Wars to

Author Ken Rogers pictured (centre) with members of the 'Lost Tribe' at one of the hugely popular Everton & Scottie Road street reunions in Everton Park

become a *breed* apart; a *multitude* of tough, proud, committed and welcoming individuals who remain proud of their *genealogy* as *natives* of a unique inner city environment where the word *community* was something everyone understood and respected.

That lady missed the point, but four reprints later, I feel the first 'Lost Tribe of Everton & Scottie Road' book struck a meaningful chord with the people who understood its aims and revelled in its message.

It was about a slum clearance programme that I described as being of almost biblical proportions. 125,000 people bulldozed to the outer limits of the city or used in a High Rise experiment that most people now accept was ill-conceived at its best and a panic solution at its worst.

It was a vision implemented by planners who went home to middle class suburbia without having to deal with the consequences of being isolated on a tenth floor landing with broken lifts, graffiti and communal areas that inspired vandalism. Most significantly, families and friends, used to a century of open-door community living, lost the fundamental ability to meet in the street, stop for a chat, shout over a backyard wall for help, or at a much more simplistic level, help each other out like good neighbours do.

I genuinely tried to look at every side of the argument as I worked my way through the original 'Lost Tribe of Everton & Scottie Road' book.

Every word I typed helped me feel the warmth of an open fire; the chill (and excitement) of standing underneath a house in a cavernous dark cellar; the smell of the washing hanging on a rack in the kitchen; the shaft of sunlight at the end of a dark lobby; the noise of kids outside playing Tick or Alalio; and the thud of a plastic football on a gable wall.

'Mam, I'm going out to play. See you when it's dark . . . '

'A GOOD SEWER IS FAR NOBLER AND FAR HOLIER THAN THE MOST ADMIRED MADONNA EVER PAINTED'

You have to go a long way to top the single sentence uttered by the great Victorian artist and art critic John Ruskin

John Ruskin saw an artistic reverence in our sewers

AS a lifelong journalist, I love a good quote. Irish writer and poet Oscar Wilde, never far from the headlines in Victorian England, would have been a media and television superstar today with such gems as: *"The books that the world calls immoral are the books that show the world its own shame"*, and *"America is the only country that went from barbarism to decadence without civilisation in between."*

German physicist Albert Einstein uttered another of my favourite one-liners: *"I don't know what weapons will be used in World War 3, but in World War 4 people will use sticks and stones."*

Absolutely brilliant! The Nobel Prize winner also had the genius during one lunch break to conjure up his world famous Theory of Relativity. Don't ask!

I should add that there was a time in the mid-1950s when the kids round our way fought out something in between World War 2 and World War 3 on the narrow Everton 'oller' or 'debris' that linked Melbourne Street and the adjacent Adelaide Street. Of course, we didn't bother with the sticks. Stone fights unfolded from time to time, but only because

15

Winston Churchill: "We will fight them on the ollers … we will never surrender!'

we each had loads of 'ammunition' on those old bomb sites. Incredibly, I can't remember anyone being hurt.

Actually, the only time I was ever on the receiving end of a missile was 'thanks' to one of my own mates. Johnny Mac used my backside for target practice one day as he fired a pellet from his air gun while enjoying the sunshine atop his backyard wall that looked down onto the aforementioned 'debris'.

I won't reveal my one-line response, but you can probably guess.

In any case, I should not make it seem like we were intent on daily war games with our street neighbours.

Peace reigned for 99.9 per cent of the time, and more often than not the 'debris' was used for a seasonal game of 'ollies' which required an intricate knowledge of parrots (coloured marbles, not birds), steelies (glorified shiny steel ball-bearings that could shift any number of 'ollies' from a hole), and bollywoshers (giant marbles of clear glass that were the

equivalent of calling out the big guns when the game got really serious).

A small and shallow circular hole would be dug in the muck where each kid would deposit an ollie.

We would step back 15 feet and, in turn, each roll another ollie towards this target. The nearest had first opportunity to try and blast those tiny coloured orbs out of the hole. Of course, you won any that popped out.

This is where the 'bollywoshers' or 'steelies' came in, much more likely to bring instant reward. But you had to be careful. If this heavy bombing tactic didn't work, you could easily lose a key bit of ammunition from your collection if it remained in the hole to become a target in its own right for a bollywosher blast from a gleeful opponent.

One bollywosher was worth at least four smaller ollies, and this instinctive valuation of each piece of your marbles collection was important, not least when it came to swapping. Of course, any heavy defeats in the world of 'ollies' would require a top-up visit to Woolies on 'Greaty' or Walton Road the following weekend.

I'm sure Albert Einstein would have had his own special theory for winning a game of 'ollies' but even the great German would have had his work cut out beating the kids in our street.

But back to my favourite all-time quote. Any idea who might have uttered it? The great Winston Churchill perhaps, whose most famous saying could so easily have been:

**"We will fight them on the ollers.
We will fight them up the back jiggers.
We will fight them in the Scottie Road
ale houses and in Greaty's corner
shops. We will NEVER surrender."**

Hitler's Storm Troopers wouldn't have lasted five minutes trying to capture Mount Everton (or any part of Liverpool). In our street, a thousand Johnny Macs would have been there with their air guns, catapults and bows and arrows. We would have been storing a cache of bricks in the back entry middens where the smell alone would have been more deadly than a consignment of mustard gas.

I would have been straight into battle proudly carrying the wooden shield with its King Arthur style motif, and the wooden sword, made for me by my uncle Bobby Wareing. Those Germans wouldn't have stood a chance.

But I digress. I must return to the theme of my favourite quotes, quickly ruling out obvious contenders from the lips of giants like Churchill *(We make a living by what we get, but we make a life by what we give)*; Abraham Lincoln *(As I would not be a slave, so I would not be a master. This expresses my idea of democracy)*;

John F. Kennedy *(Ask not what your country can do for you. Ask what you can do for your country)*; Nelson Mandela *(Education is the most powerful weapon you can use to change the world)*.

Or even sporting legends like Muhammad Ali *(I float like a butterfly and sting like a bee)*; and Bill Shankly *(Football is not a matter of life or death, it is much more important than that)*.

For me, you have to go a long way to top the single sentence uttered by the great Victorian artist and art critic John Ruskin who declared:

**"A good sewer is far nobler and
far holier than the most admired
Madonna ever painted."**

Do you know something? He is absolutely right. Where would we have been without the Victorian sewers that swept down in straight lines under the steep terraced streets of Everton and Scottie Road? Can you even begin to imagine this wonderland of secret tunnels and caverns, from the summit of Mount Everton to some distant outlet in the Docks?

I admire and respect Ruskin's wise words. I'm only sorry that he didn't also turn his descriptive thoughts to the merits of back entries, backyards, old street lamps, street games, the oller and the debris, attics, parlours, scrubbed clean front steps, open doors, bin men, rag and bone men, kids, cats and dogs . . .

No problem. I'm more than happy to pick up on these subjects on your behalf and with your help, reporting from the heart of inner city Liverpool circa 1948-1962.

Albert Einstein's wise words: "I don't know what weapons will be used in World War 3, but in World War 4 people will use sticks and stones!"

A young girl entertains the regulars in a
Scottie Road pub, early in the last century

THE SIGHTS, SOUNDS AND SMELLS OF THE OLD AND ORIGINAL SCOTTIE ROAD THAT DROVE ONE FAMILY TO NEW YORK

Scotland Road and its legendary old streets has been the subject of some remarkable family history research within the United States

THE 'Lost Tribe of Everton & Scottie Road' book attracted interest from all over the world, highlighting the huge on-going interest in the famous old inner city districts of Liverpool.

Indeed, Scotland Road and its legendary old streets has been the subject of some remarkable family history research within the United States cities of Kansas and Oklahoma where John Deford has been investigating his Liverpool family roots.

John's focus has been specifically on Hopwood Street on the east side of 'Scottie' and it struck a personal chord with me because this is where, in 1880, my great great grandparents Peter and Maria Rogers resided, surrounded by the old court houses. My great grandfather Thomas McLoughlin Rogers also lived at numbers 133 and 88.

John Deford's family research revealed that his ancestors, Stephen and Elisabeth Walch (nee Charnock), were born in England in the early 1820s. They lived in Hopwood Street for four years up to 1850 before emigrating to New York in the spring of 1851. They eventually settled in Hastings-on-Hudson, New York, where they raised seven children.

Their offspring would settle in Kansas and Oklahoma, where many of their descendents still live today.

John has original letters from Stephen and Elisabeth that graphically describe the Scotland Road area and Hopwood Street in particular . . .

July 23, 1850 . . .

"Last night there were thunderstorms and heavy rains. Thank God! The rain helped to wash down the grime and the stench of human garbage and waste.

"They say you get used to the smell if you live here long enough. But on a hot and humid day, like yesterday, the smell is overwhelming. Let's hope a cooler western wind prevails over the Liverpool port today.

"We woke up to the cry of our newest cousin, seven-month-old Margaret Walch who was born on the 27th of January of this year. She is called Maggie. Her 2½ -year-old brother, Jimmie Walch, is also up and playing on the floor with a small wooden boat his father made from scrap lumber."

Stephen Walch and Elisabeth Charnock first came to the Scotland Road area in 1846 when they were married at St. Nicholas, the church for seamen at the Pier Head. Stephen was a stone-getter at a local quarry. The Walch family provide us with a remarkable personal image of the area at that time.

"It was early evening as we turned south on Scotland Road which runs along what once was the old coach route from the town centre of Liverpool to the north. The locals call it Scottie Road. As we walked down Scottie, we passed scores of workshops, pubs, and doss houses.

"The sidewalk merchants were selling goods of every description and kind, including themselves.

"The road was teeming with people – beggars, hawkers, drunks and people just coming and going. The narrow side streets are packed with poorly built cramped houses, many of which are crammed into dark courts. Hopwood Street is no exception. Hopwood is about eight blocks long, stretching between Scotland Road and Vauxhall. Three blocks beyond Vauxhall is the port of Liverpool."

The population of Liverpool from 1841 to 1851 had skyrocketed to 367,000. This was primarily due to the Irish Potato Famine of the 1840s. 1847 was the peak year when hundreds of thousands of desperate Irish arrived in Liverpool on the so-called 'coffin' ships. Many went on to America, but many others remained in the city because they could not afford the onward passage.

These Irish families crammed into the nooks, crannies and basements of the houses and tenement buildings between Scotland Road and Vauxhall Road, alongside the native working class of Liverpool and an in-bound workforce from the surrounding areas of Merseyside and beyond.

These included my great great grandfather, Peter Rogers, who arrived here from the Cheshire salt mining town of Northwich, and my great great grandmother Maria Hutchinson who came from much further afield, Nottingham.

The strip of land between Scottie Road and Vauxhall Road was said to be the most densely populated in the civilised world and people in its streets were linked by two words – 'abject poverty'.

These words drew the tightly-packed neighbours together, and this is how two other even more important words came into our psyche – *community spirit.*

Our forefathers had to stand together to survive . . .

However, the letters of the Walch family highlight an inevitable consequence of thousands of people living cheek by jowl in those challenging mid-1800s courts and terraced houses.

"The boom creates its own special excitement, but it also fosters cholera and typhus. The proliferation of diseases, the poverty, cold and hunger prompts one health official to declare Liverpool to be the unhealthiest town in England at this time."

It is of little wonder that Elisabeth and Stephen Walch looked for a new place to raise their fledgling family (the United States).

They escaped to the New World. My family and thousands of others remained to create their own New World on the slopes of Everton and its surrounding districts.

I have managed to research all of the Liverpool streets the Rogers family lived in over a period of 110 years between 1852 and 1962 when the demolition derby finally over-ran our final residence in heartland Netherfield Road North (see right).

It's not the designer wear today's kids demand. These barefoot ragged boys make do in the early 1900s near a Scottie Road pub

Peter and Maria Rogers (nee Hutchinson), my great great grandparents:

1852: Moorfields, close to the original Tithebarn Street Railway Station (1850), that eight years later was renamed Exchange Station.

1853: 4 Court, Tatlock Street (off Vauxhall Road), where my great grandfather Thomas McLoughlin Rogers was born.

1861: 7 Aspinall Street, Kirkdale.

1871: 78 Selwyn Street, Kirkdale.

1881: 133 Hopwood Street (off Scotland Road).

At this time, the family of my great grandmother Margaret (Morrison) Rogers also lived in Hopwood Street at number 88 with her parents Daniel and Mary. Part of the street still stands with the Parrot Pub now sadly closed on its corner with 'Scottie' – but the original court houses have long since gone.

Thomas McLoughlin Rogers and Margaret Rogers (nee Morrison), my great grandparents:

1890: 66 Ruskin Street, Kirkdale, where my grandfather Thomas was born.
1893: 56 Pugin Street, Walton.
1901: 66 Beacon Lane, Everton.
1911: 24 Calder Street, Everton.
1919: 12 Copeland Street, Everton.

Thomas and Emily Rogers (nee McGowan):

1920: As above until slum clearance saw the house demolished around 1963.

Harry and May Rogers (nee Wareing):

1949: 8 Melbourne Street, Everton (until the slum clearance development in 1962).

That's four generations and eleven properties in just over a century in a fairly tight geographic area. It involved a journey from the city centre up to Vauxhall Road, with a sortie to Kirkdale and Walton before returning to the heart of Scotland Road.

My family finally moved up onto Everton's famous hill after a spell in Walton – the district that is, not HM Prison!

It's intriguing to map out your roots and if you haven't done so, you should really try. It gives you a real sense of where you come from and aligns you forever with a group of like-minded people who might be strangers when you first meet, but who feel like a band of brothers and sisters within minutes of discussing familiar district landmarks like schools, churches and shops.

Stephen and Elisabeth Walch might have found their New World in the United States after leaving Scotland Road.

I'm proud that my family decided that their future was much closer to home and used Scottie Road as a platform to build their own new Everton dawn.

The poverty of the original Scottie Road as a lady sleeps rough with a shawl her only comfort

A local character gets a little help on 'Greaty' from a boy who was his eyes and ears in Edwardian Liverpool

A busy start to the day at the famous open air market at the end of Great Homer Street

'WE SHALL FIGHT THEM ON THE BEACHES, WE WILL FIGHT THEM IN' THE STABLES OF SCOTTIE...

Horses were once crucial to the working life of every big town and city

WHILE I've continued to research the social history of the Everton and Scotland Road area, I have already made it clear that my second 'Lost Tribe' book majors on the very personal street memories that people have been sending me over the past year and a half.

I wanted to get into them very quickly in this edition because these personal thoughts are worth more than thousands of words of academic research.

Jimmy Doran from Norris Green was an early contributor to my Liverpool Echo Saturday column. He wrote:

"I have been reading the 'Lost Tribe of Everton & Scottie Road' book and there was mention of Mould Street off Scotland Road where I was born at number 7 in 1931. It was a great street to live in because it had four stables and so I grew up around horses. I worked for John Taylor & Son, team owners.

"I started off as a pony lad, and during the Second World War the Germans blitzed all our schools and houses with their heavy bombing.

"The famous Rotunda Theatre was at the top of our street (three storeys high and standing on

The old stables on Mould Street

the triangle between Scottie Road, Stanley Road, and Boundary Street). It was hit with fire bombs during an air raid. It burned to the ground and the fire spread to Waugh's Funeral Stables next door.

"All the men, woman, and the Air Raid Wardens, including my dad and my old boss Dick Clensy, John Tart, and Tommy Wright, all came to give a hand and get the flames out.

"I got some ropes and put all the horses by the Air Raid Shelters to keep them safe and out of the way until the Animal Rescue people came the next morning, and so the old Rotunda burned to the ground with all the horses safe.

"Everyone was made up, but all of the old women in our street were moaning about the horse muck. My dad went mad and shouted at them to go and get their brushes and shovels to clean it up, which some of them did.

"They knew what a brave thing the men had done. My Aunt Sally even wrote to Mr. Winston Churchill about it, but she never got a reply. It was a brave thing from the Scottie Roaders of Mould Street."

Brave indeed, Jimmy, and just one of the many stories sent to me about horses in the Everton and Scotland Road area.

Indeed, I well recall that two of my mother's brothers, Alan (Adam) and Bobby Wareing, worked for the Co-op which actually had stables on Walton Road behind the old Co-op store (opposite what was the famous Frost's department store where my mother worked, now the Thomas Frost Bar).

I got my first rubber-soled football boots at the Walton Road Co-op and the fact that the legendary Stanley Matthews had his name on them pinpoints the era to the mid 1950s.

My uncles would go to the Co-op stables each morning and hitch their horses up to the famous box-shaped bread vans. These horses didn't need any local map or human guidance, setting off immediately on their tried and trusted routes and stopping instinctively outside every house that had a bread or cake order.

I used to be thrilled to be able to join my Uncle Alan and take the reins, imagining I was leading a Wagon Train across the prairies of America.

Back at the stables, we would meet up with Uncle Bobby and he would amuse us by unsaddling his horse and riding it bare back around the cobbled yard.

My cousin Alan won't mind me telling the story about his father's funeral. Everyone was trying to keep it together as we listened to a very moving tribute to my Uncle Alan because he was such a wonderful man, always very calm and sensible about everything.

Whoever was giving the church homily suddenly made reference to my uncle's working days at the Co-op and Beauty, his favourite old horse.

His brother and fellow Co-op horseman and van driver Bobby, who had managed to keep his feelings firmly under wraps until this point, suddenly lost it completely and the tears were unstoppable.

So, those days with Beauty and the rest, amidst the tackle and the Co-op vans in a small stable in Walton Road, must have held some very special and personal memories.

There are some great stories to come about people who delivered goods and services into the very heart of our communities.

Meanwhile, as I continued my own family research, it was fitting to find out that Uncle

A powerful working horse in all its finery with its fiercely proud owner

Alan and Uncle Bobby's own grandfather, another Bob Wareing, was actually a fully trained Ostler who had looked after the horses and stage coaches at the famous Royal Goat Hotel in Beddgelert, North Wales.

Maybe I could still take a Wagon Train west after all, in honour of my great grandfather on my mother's side, and the Wareing horsemen of Everton!

Of course, horses were once crucial to the working life of every big town and city. The Retired Carters' Association is fiercely proud of its connections with the inner city working horses of Liverpool.

They began an appeal, in 1997, to raise money for a permanent monument to the city's horses. On 1 May 2010, Lord Mayor of Liverpool, Mike Storey, unveiled a life size figure of a working horse by artist Judy Boyt at a prominent site close to the Maritime Museum and the new Museum of Liverpool.

The sculpture, entitled 'Waiting', depicts a working dock horse ready to set off on its next journey. The date chosen for the ceremony was special, coinciding with the traditional date of the May Day horse parades.

A plaque honouring Liverpool's carters and their horses is also in place on the wall of the Throstle's Nest Pub on Scotland Road, another fitting and important tribute.

The shores of Llyn Dinas, near Beddgelert. Inset, an old picture of the village of Beddgelert

FROM PICTURESQUE SNOWDONIA TO A SAD END IN EVERTON'S DENSELY PACKED CONCRETE JUNGLE

Work was more plentiful in a bustling inner city district than might have been on offer in the sleepy Welsh village my great grandparents left behind

IN the last chapter, I mentioned the North Wales village of Beddgelert. For a while, in the late 1800s, my great great grandfather Bob Wareing, an Everton man, was an ostler at the local Goat Hotel.

Beddgelert, for me, is one of the most beautiful villages in Wales, nestling behind the Snowdonia mountain range.

Despite the village's dramatic position, surrounded by hills and with a crystal clear river meandering through it, I assume the main attraction for Bob Wareing was not the inspiring views, but rather a young local girl named Ellen Williams.

In 1879, Bob and Ellen married. Ellen recorded her address as Tan y Graig, Dolfriarg. 'Tan y Graig' means 'below the rock, or cliff' which is not surprising because many of the houses and cottages in this dramatic area are built under towering rock outcrops.

Bob confirmed his lodgings as the Goat Hotel, later renamed the Royal Goat Hotel after visits by Royal relatives of Queen Victoria.

I mentioned that Bob was an ostler, looking after the horses that brought stage coaches to the hotel. He would have been extremely comfortable around animals of any sort. His father John Wareing was a gamekeeper, a person who looked after an area of countryside to make sure there was enough game for shooting.

Bob was 27 at this time and his bride-to-be, Ellen, was seven years younger.

Their wedding took place at Beddgelert's historic St. Mary's Church on 15 October, 1879, conducted by the Rev. Richard Williams whose name is remembered in a plaque that can still be seen on the church wall.

Within two years (1881 Wales census), Bob and Ellen were now living in the heart of Beddgelert at 101 Ty'r Ysgoldy, with William Williams aged 78 (described as a Shoemaker) and his wife Ellen Williams (62) living next door at 100 Ty'r Ysgoldy. William and Ellen Snr. were almost certainly young Ellen's grandparents.

By now Robert was describing himself on the census as an Indoor Servant. Ellen's brother, Slate Miner Robert Williams, was living with them.

By 1891, Bob Wareing had taken the decision to return to Liverpool, second city of the Empire at that time. He was living with Ellen and sons Robert, John and Adam (my grandfather) at Brown's Buildings, 19 Prince Edwin Street, Everton.

The 1892 census now describes Bob as a general labourer (clearly not many stage coaches and horses to look after in 'Prinny Eddy' at that time).

However, work was clearly more plentiful in a bustling inner city district than might have been on offer in the sleepy village he had left behind.

The outlook from this highly built up area with its steep terraced streets and tightly-packed back to back houses must have been a dramatic change for Ellen in particular.

She battled on, coping with five children, but it all ended in tragic circumstances in October, 1899.

Ellen, aged just 38, was badly scalded by water from a boiling kettle on an old kitchen

Number 6 Court, Prince Edwin Street

range with its open fire. She was rushed to Mill Road Infirmary, but never recovered from this dreadful incident. This must have been a disastrous scenario for the emerging Wareing family.

I'm sure Ellen had constantly missed her picturesque Beddgelert childhood home, nestling amongst those imposing mountains of Snowdonia which, ironically, she would have seen in the far distance every time she looked across the Mersey on a clear day from her new Everton surroundings.

No doubt she had told her boys, including my grandfather Adam, the famous legend of Gelert:

In the 13th Century, Llewlyn, Prince of North Wales, had a palace in the Snowdon area. One day he went hunting without his faithful hound Gelert, who appeared to have gone missing.

On the Prince's return, Gelert joyfully sprang out to greet his master. The hound was smeared with blood.

The Prince, alarmed, hastened to find his son, and saw the infant's cot empty, the bedclothes and floor covered in blood. The frantic Prince plunged his sword into Gelert's side, thinking the hound had killed his heir.

The dog's dying yelp was answered by a child's cry.

Llewelyn searched and discovered the boy unharmed, but nearby was the body of a great wolf that Gelert had slain. Llewelyn is said to have never smiled again, and he buried Gelert with honour in a field close to the village where the memorial can still be seen. Beddgelert, in English, means "Gelert's Grave".

It was with real sadness that my research revealed the untimely death of my great great grandmother Ellen Wareing.

The 1902 Census reveals that Bob Wareing was now living at 49 Ellison Street, Everton with three of his sons – Robert Jnr, John and Adam.

However, there is no reference to the two younger Wareing children, George and Isabella.

Clearly, the lives of these little ones were changed forever after their mother's untimely death and their fate highlights the poverty that was prevalent in the district at that time.

It appears that Bob Wareing was forced to put George and Isabella into a Dr. Barnardo's Home, and George was then taken by ship to Canada along with a lot of other UK children. He was adopted by a family called Denny.

At 21, just before the First World War, he returned to Liverpool to seek out his sister whom he had remembered.

He did eventually find her, working for a Mr. Gladstone in London as a maid. George took Isabella back to Canada and she eventually married the son of the Denny family. The Denny / Wareings still live in Canada.

Gelert's grave at Beddgelert

In my first 'Lost Tribe' book, I revealed that my great grandmother Margaret on the Rogers' side of the family had drowned after leaping from a Mersey ferry, unable to cope after two of her sons were killed in the Great War (1914-1918). The discovery that another great grandmother had been lost in equally tragic circumstances is a painful reminder that we should take nothing for granted in life.

Ellen Wareing's dreadful accident resonated with me because of an experience I had linked with one of those old fire ranges.

As a kid in the Fifties, my grandfather had a large range in the kitchen of our house in Melbourne Street, Everton.

A kitchen chair was in front of the open fire, probably placed there to air some washing.

I sat astride it, facing the chair back that was nearest to the fire, and stupidly started to rock backwards and forwards, probably pretending I was riding Trigger, the horse of my famous cowboy hero Roy Rogers.

Suddenly, one forward rock too many pitched the chair towards the fire grate. I instinctively put out my hands to save myself and touched the hot bars across the front of the grate.

You can imagine the chaos as my parents grabbed me to give instant first aid. In those days, panic treatment for burns included putting margarine on the skin which was probably the worst thing you could do.

Anyway, unlike my great great grandmother, I survived my kitchen range incident.

I'm sure there must have been hundreds of accidents, many of them fatal, linked with the open fires that burned brightly in the kitchens of every house across the city.

They were warming, welcoming and hugely effective, but the potential for danger was always there, as any fireman from the era will confirm.

Just look at those faces ... awe, wonder, and fright as the escapades of our big screen heroes unfold at the Saturday matinee. Flash Gordon is pictured with his arch-enemy the Emperor Ming the Merciless

FLASH GORDON, MING THE MERCILESS AND THE AMAZING SATURDAY MORNING WORLD OF THE ABC MINORS

The cinemas snatched you off the streets and swept you up into a cavernous auditorium, where for a couple of hours total anarchy reigned

I ALWAYS smile when I watch re-runs of that classic TV war series 'Colditz' featuring, the notorious German castle and prisoner-of-war-camp Oflag IV-C where a band of indefatigable Allied officers continually plotted and planned a series of audacious escapes during the Second World War.

As a youngster, born three years after the end of the hostilities, I always felt as if we were inspired to reverse the Colditz escape mentality every Saturday morning as we tried to break into the formidable, dark and 'dangerous' environs of our local Liverpool picture houses – intent on sharing in the adventures of the super heroes who inspired us from the big screens.

I wrote about this in one of the Liverpool Echo's highly popular heritage magazines entitled 'The Lost Cinemas of Liverpool', recalling that in Colditz, a searchlight beam would sweep the courtyards and alleyways of the imposing castle, looking to capture any sign of an impending break-out.

In the cinemas of inner city Liverpool, the torches and eagle eyes of the uniformed usherettes would be scouring the darkness for signs of an impending break-in! The Oflag IV-C prisoners came up with many

ideas to escape from within the imposing surroundings of Colditz castle. The kids of the Saturday Matinee were equally audacious. They would crawl on their stomachs under rows of seats and down dark passageways to reach their goal, the Exit Doors with their push-bar release mechanisms. Suddenly a shaft of sunlight would pierce the darkness in the corner of the building, and kids would scramble in for a free show, disappearing into the shadows as torch beams flashed across the seats to try and identify the intruders. It was all a game, an integral part of the show. After all, we were all fully paid up members of the 'ABC Minors Club' and as such were the future of the cinemas, although movie mania would soon be seriously threatened by the new entertainment wonder, a flickering box in the corner of every living room known as the TV.

But at the start of the 1950s, the cinema was still the king and queen of our entertainment world, not least in the ABC Cinemas that dominated every big British city.

ABC was established in 1927 by solicitor John Maxwell and by 1945 it operated over 400 cinemas nationwide and was second only to Rank's Odeon chain. ABC set up the first major Saturday cinema club for children, the 'ABC Minors'. At the beginning of each Saturday morning session, the 'Minors Song' would be played to the tune of 'Blaze Away' by Abe Holzmann (1874–1939), with the lyrics presented on the screen with a bouncing red ball above the words to help and inspire the young audience. Hundreds of high-pitched voices would sing:

We are the boys and girls well known as
Minors of the ABC
And every Saturday all line up
To see the films we like
And shout aloud with glee
We love to laugh and have a sing-song
Just a happy crowd are we
We're all pals together
We're minors of the ABC

The famous Everton Palace Cinema, Everton Road

Let's be clear. Going to the 'flicks' or the 'pics' to see a Saturday morning kids' matinee was almost as daunting an experience as venturing into the tight confines of one of the caged Boys' Pens at our famous city football grounds, where you took your life in your own hands amidst a screaming, heaving mass of teenage testosterone.

The cinemas, with their mysterious passages and staircases, snatched you off the streets on a bright Mersey Saturday morning and swept you up into the total blackness of a cavernous auditorium where, for a couple of hours, total anarchy reigned, interspersed by moments of sheer movie magic.

Kids will be kids in any environment, but plunge them into semi darkness with a license to cause mini mayhem whilst revelling in the adventures of their screen heroes and you have the recipe for a cauldron of excitement and action, on and off the screen.

My cinema super hero was Flash Gordon, matched only by my comic hero Dan Dare. I had Dan Dare wallpaper adorning the bedroom walls in our Everton terraced house and every night I played out a sci-fi adventure alongside Dan, defending Planet Earth from The Mekon, the super-intelligent ruler of the Treens.

This would take on a whole new meaning every Saturday morning when I visited either the Popular Cinema (The Pop) on Netherfield Road North or the Astoria on

All change on Netherfield Road.
The 'Pop' cinema stands forlorn up the hill

The Astoria Cinema on
Walton Road – now demolished

Walton Road where Flash Gordon had his regular big screen battles with Emperor Ming the Merciless.

Kids were captivated by these outer space adventures which unfolded week by week, always leaving us with a terrifying cliff-hanger.

Flash would be up to his neck in a giant tank of water. Ming would instruct his space age accomplices to slam the lid shut and we would see the water rising above Flash's head with no means of escape. Then we would hear those words: *"Will Flash Gordon escape his watery Tomb of Death? Will our hero live to fight another day?"*

Of course, the next week's film would start with Flash up to his waist in water and always manipulating his escape from the furious Ming.

But it was the uncertainty and sheer excitement of it all that kept drawing us back for our next fix of Saturday morning madness.

My father worked in a number of Liverpool cinemas and so I was able to go behind the scenes and witness the technicalities of the Projection Room.

I always found cinemas to be ghostly places once their audiences had disappeared into the night, leaving the buildings strangely silent and empty while minutes earlier the sights and sounds of the movie adventures had been absolutely spell-binding. Never mind Phantom of the Opera. Andrew Lloyd Webber could easily have written Phantom of the Astoria!

When they eventually closed down 'The Pop' in the late 1950s, I can remember being one of an army of young local boys who could not wait to get into the empty and now derelict building, marauding up and down the old staircases and passageways and even climbing high up into the roof space.

I recall that two tramline joists had been exposed, stretching from the back of the cinema at roof level to a position high above what had previously been the big screen, probably 30 or 40 feet in the air.

With a knee on each of these joists, I edged forward to traverse above my former picture house domain. All the kids were daring each other to do it.

Those joists could have been rotten and we could have all plunged into the first row of the pit, but we did it in the name of Flash, Hopalong Cassidy, Roy Rogers and the rest.

I could almost hear the cliff-hanging teaser: *"Will young Kenny Rogers escape? Will he traverse the joists of death like his hero Flash before him and make it to Planet Everton on the other side? Don't miss next week's exciting episode of . . . The Demise of the Pop Cinema, and the Magical World of the ABC Minors."*

Many of the old cinemas could also be very basic and, in researching my book 'The Lost Tribe of Everton and Scottie Road' I found out that in the dark days of the Depression in the 1930s, it wasn't just money that gained you entry into Liverpool cinemas.

My own father recalls going to the old picture house in Everton Road and gaining entry by handing over a couple of jam jars, something confirmed to me by Terry Cooke, a fellow local author. Terry told me: *"There were two cinemas in our area, one the respectable 'Roscommon' where they had a doorman who demanded you had cash. Then there was the 'Tivoli' with its wooden seats. It was a deplorable place, but loved by many. They would let you in for three or four jam jars."*

The modern multiplexes somehow don't cut it for me. It's like watching a film in your living room. A visit to the 'pics' from the Thirties to the Sixties was not just about the films, but rather an exciting, amazing experience, often in an art deco environment of true glamour. Sadly, we will never again see the likes of these Picture Palaces of the past.

Going to the cinema wasn't just about the fantastic epic films that captured our imagination. It was very much an experience, equal to that of going to some of the great theatres. The cinema builders ensured this was the case by building Picture Palaces that oozed with magic because of the sheer luxury and the décor.

Some of the souvenir programmes available at that time sum up the whole mood of going to the pictures in the Fifties and Sixties.

These publications were produced to support massive blockbusters and were not made available for every movie.

However, some of the really classic film productions clearly justified high quality printed souvenir programmes which became collectors' items in their own right. They featured information on the production staff as well as the stars and gave an insight into how the films were made.

Many of the major films at this time were over three hours long and this inspired the practice of having a very civilised formal intermission during which cinema goers could have refreshments and discuss the quality of the performance before returning to see the final part.

Liverpool had its share of specialist picture houses. The Tatler in Church Street majored on cartoons and was a magnet for kids from all over the city. The News Theatre on Clayton Square showed short and highly stylised news reels from the world famous Pathé News stable. These were the days, of course, before 24 hour news on the TV.

People would be able to see footage of events like the Grand National or the FA Cup Final for the first time on any sort of screen. The power of the cinema was highlighted by the fact that the Liverpool Echo front page, rather than being totally news-driven, was dominated by advertising, mainly featuring local cinemas.

The local cinemas in the Everton, Scottie Road and surrounding areas included:

Astoria, Walton Road; *Commodore*, Stanley Road; *Cosy Cinema*, Boaler Street; *Derby*, Scotland Road; *The Everton*, Heyworth Street; *Gaiety*, Scotland Road; *Garrick*, Westminster Road; *Gaumont Palace*, Oakfield Road; *The Gem*, Vescock Street; *Grosvenor*, Stanley Road; *Homer*, Great Homer Street; *Imperial*, Stanley Road; *Liverpool Palladium*, West Derby Road; *Liverpool Picturedrome*, Kensington; *Lytton*, Lytton Street; *Majestic Picture Palace*, Daulby Street; *Mere Lane Super Cinema*, Mere Lane; *Popular*, Netherfield Road North; *Princess*, Selwyn Street; *Queen's*, Walton Road; *Roscommon Cinema*, Roscommon Street; *Royal*, Breck Road; *Royal Hippodrome*, West Derby Road; *Savoy Picture Theatre*, West Derby Road; *Tivoli*, Roscommon Street; *Victory Picture House*, Walton Road.

Source: *Kelly's Trades Directory, 1958*

DERELICT SITES HOLD SECRETS TO EVERTON'S THEATRES OF DREAMS LIKE THE LYRIC AND ROTUNDA

I was never bored because Liverpool 5, with its famous roads and steep streets, was such a remarkable place to explore

AS a young boy, I never missed an opportunity to investigate every inch of the district I was brought up in. I was like a taxi driver doing the 'knowledge' — without the taxi!

I wanted to know the name of every street, understand every short cut to get there, try out every playground, and generally build up a powerful mental picture of the area where my father, grandfather, great grandfather, and great great grandfather had brought up successive generations of the Rogers family.

I was never bored because Liverpool 5, with its famous roads and steep streets, was such a remarkable place to live and explore. Every now and then I would come across something that really captured my attention, or that I never fully understood.

For instance, whenever I found myself in Alvina Lane, a non-descript back street between the more famous Everton Valley and

Walton Road, I was always fascinated by what was clearly the back wall of an old building whose frontage had clearly been on the Valley itself.

In reality, it wasn't very special, except for an inscription above an old entrance that leapt out at you . . . STAGE DOOR.

I'm sure that the site was being used at this time as a garage or storage facility for demolition firm Rainfords because I remember large trucks going in and out. But what about that sign, suggesting this was originally an old theatre?

What I could not have known as a young boy was that I was looking at the site of a former auditorium, built in 1897, that could accommodate a seated audience of up to 2,000 people. This was Everton's famous Lyric Theatre and apart from that Stage Door sign, there was little else to suggest that this had

Dramatic theatre advertising posters on an inner city street corner billboard captivated the public.
Opposite page: Everton's famous Lyric Theatre which stood on Everton Valley

been a hugely popular local entertainments venue.

These days, when most people turn up the steep gradient that is Everton Valley, many of them on their way to our two modern theatres of dreams – Goodison Park and Anfield – they simply have no idea that a major theatre once fronted out onto the Valley on the left hand side.

Ellis Brammall Jnr. was the man who launched the Lyric when Queen Victoria was still on the throne. His other claim to fame was linked with the even more well known Shakespeare Theatre in Fraser Street off London Road. The Lyric's impressive frontage of terracotta brick work with three large arched entrance doors led theatre goers into a large foyer that featured an electric light candelabra, hugely impressive at the time. At first floor level, five arched windows looked out across Everton Valley. The venue was served by the tram system although most customers were drawn from the densely populated local streets. The side wall, facing down the hill towards the junction of Netherfield Road North, Kirkdale Road, and Walton Road, carried a massive painted 'LYRIC THEATRE' sign. A more decorative sign was positioned high above the first floor window arches on the Valley frontage.

The excellent book 'Liverpool Stage' by Harold Ackroyd reveals that inside the auditorium the ceiling was dotted all over with electric lights. Curved fronted boxes were either side of the impressive dress circle. The Lyric opened on Boxing Day 1897 with two performances of the pantomime Blue Beard.

The boxes could be booked in advance for one guinea (21 shillings, or £1 and 5 pence in modern money) which would have been a king's ransom for most people at that time. The orchestra stall seats were two shillings (ten pence), the circle seats one shilling and sixpence and the gallery sixpence.

The Lyric mainly staged variety shows, with occasional plays. But the advent of the cinemas challenged the audience numbers and the theatre itself had to move with the times, renovated to become the Lyric Super Cinema in 1921. However, even this venture was shortlived and no application was made to renew the cinematograph license in 1924.

Another refurbishment followed in 1925 when 'live' entertainment returned with a revue entitled 'There You Are Then!'

Famous Liverpool comedian Ted Ray appeared at the Lyric in 1927 for £7 a week. But when the Liverpool Fire Brigade produced a report suggesting that there was a hazard because of unsatisfactory exit points, the theatre closed for the last time on 19 November 1932.

The building was used as a warehouse, only to be destroyed by enemy bombing in the Second World War. The site would then be used by Rainfords, which brings the story up to date with my fascination for the 'Stage Door' sign at the back. Harold Ackroyd also indicates that the words '6.40 Twice Nightly 8.85' were painted on that remaining wall.

I just know that it was a thrilling thought for a young boy that a major theatre had existed on this site with all the magic this conjured up.

Another site that continues to fascinate me, the destruction of which is referred to in an earlier chapter, is just over half a mile away down the hill on that famous triangular piece of ground at the junction of Scotland Road and Stanley Road – the Rotunda.

Everyone knows where it is, but unless you are of a certain age, you possibly don't know its rich theatre history. As a kid, I always saw the 'Rotunda' as a famous tram and bus junction. Indeed, the name is burned into my mind because my father was once knocked down there by a motor bike early one morning, although he lived to tell the tale.

The doctors' surgery I attended as a boy – run by people like Dr. O'Brien, Dr. Smart and Dr. Sytner – was directly opposite what would have been the back of the old theatre on Boundary Street.

But the Rotunda has always been derelict in my living memory, the building having been completely destroyed by German bombs on 21st September, 1940.

An old pub, renowned for its local vocalists, was the starting point for entertainment on the site in 1863. A more extensive upper floor soon accommodated a bigger stage and, after further construction work, the Rotunda Music Hall was opened in November, 1869.

First class artistes were engaged and the Rotunda's pantomime season was renowned. The theatre also staged many successful plays, and as its popularity grew, a new gallery, balcony, stage and private boxes were erected.

However, disaster struck when the theatre burned down in 1877. Ironically, this opened up the opportunity for the well know proprietor, Dennis Grannell, to plan an even bigger and grander theatre on the site. The end product was the impressive five-storey triangular building that became such an important local landmark until that Second World War enemy air raid brought the curtain down on 62 years of almost continuous production.

Once again, 'Liverpool Stage' author Harold Ackroyd reminds us of the Rotunda's splendid facilities. Above ground level, the frontage was of the kind of mixed light and dark brick used in many of the extremely large and impressive main road public houses in the area.

Internally there were two bowling alleys in the basement; the ground floor featured the foyer, a billiard room and a public house (at the curved Scotland Road end); staircases from the foyer led up to the first floor stalls, and the landings continued up to the dress circle, amphicircle and gallery. The theatre capacity was 1,790. Not surprisingly (this was the Scottie Road area) a licensed bar was provided at the rear on all floors except for the gallery.

The interior was reconstructed in 1899 after the theatre was acquired by the famous Bent's Brewery Company. The Rotunda became a leading provincial centre for melodrama, but the entertainment package was varied, and legendary comedian Robb Wilton was a star attraction as the call grew for more light entertainment.

June Woodall revealed that her grandma was once thrown out of the Rotunda for protesting about a First World War play. June recalls:

"It was in the early 1920s and she went to see a production about the war (which ended in 1918 and was still uppermost in the thoughts of the entire nation). Grandma took exception to it and stood up and called the actors 'traitors'.

"She started to shout about how her husband had been 'gassed' and that most of the audience had sons killed and injured. Some of the audience applauded and others told her to 'pipe down'.

"A crowd gathered around her and the manager was sent for. He politely asked her to leave as she was causing a disturbance. Grandma said she would go, but under protest. She always said that she would never set foot in the theatre again. I would imagine the manager breathed a sigh of relief after that!"

I would be fascinated to know what the play was called and if it was somehow being sympathetic to German wartime soldiers while also highlighting the harrowing experiences of our troops. Clearly, it got June's grandma in a state.

What is beyond doubt are the First World War casualty numbers. The British Army recorded up to 1.6 million wounded, with 662,000 killed and 140,000 recorded as dead

or missing. That war play was a brave thing to do in a city in which tensions were clearly still running high.

It sounds like June's grandma had the makings of an inner city suffragette. I'm only surprised she did not chain herself to an immovable object inside the theatre.

Of course, the Rotunda, like the Lyric, was a huge source of entertainment for local people and most shows lifted the spirits with pantomimes and reviews within the mix. However, I would have been standing behind June's battling grandmother, not in front of her!

It was the unique appearance of the building, with its distinctive flat iron shape, that made it so impressive. The site, while famous for simply being the 'Rotunda', feels slightly sad today.

But what a venue it must have been in an era when the district had many such entertainment establishments, listed below:

1832-1865: Zoological Gardens Theatre, West Derby Road

1842: The Prince of Wales Theatre, Vauxhall Road

1861: The Casino, Princess Theatre, Bevington Hill

1869-1940: Rotunda Music Hall; Rotunda Theatre, Scotland Road.

1882: The Haymarket Music Hall, Beau Street.

1887: The Westminster Music Hall, Kirkdale.

1892: The Roscommon Music Hall/ Roscommon Picture Palace, Roscommon Street.

1897-1932: Lyric Theatre, Everton Valley.

1902-1931: The Royal Hippodrome Theatre, West Derby Road.

1905-1925: Olympia Theatre, West Derby Road.

Of course, some of these old theatres would eventually succumb to the age of the movies and re-open in different guises.

One for the family album, as these youngsters
saddle up for a donkey ride in 1955

CHAPTER 8

THE REAL MAGIC KINGDOM – VIA A THRILLING FERRY RIDE ACROSS THE RIVER MERSEY

As a boy, I felt privileged that at night I could see the coloured lights of New Brighton from where I lived

THE Mersey Ferries have been an integral part of my life. As a young boy, I journeyed on them to the seaside paradise of New Brighton.

As a teenager, I performed on the famous Royal Iris as a member of a local pop group called The Circulation with fellow band members Alan Simon, John Tetlow, Tom McDermott, and John Carney.

As an adult, I travelled to work every day using the Ferries as a very special mode of transport. It's not surprising that the Ferries have always had a fatal fascination for me.

However, I didn't understand the true relevance of the word 'fatal' until last summer as I researched my first 'The Lost Tribe of Everton & Scottie Road' book and discovered that my great grandmother, Margaret Rogers, was actually reported missing off a ferry in April, 1921, something I touched on in Chapter 5.

Aged 63, she was eventually recovered from under the Woodside Landing Stage and while the subsequent inquest declared an 'Open Verdict', it was clear that she had struggled to come to terms with a series of

First World War family tragedies relating to her sons.

So having unearthed this shocking fact, is it still possible for me to look at the Ferries in anything other than a tragic way ahead of the 91st anniversary of her death?

The fact is, I can never get away from the Ferries – nor will I ever want to. They have been an eventful, magical part of my life. Even as I write this, looking down on the famous river from the Liverpool Echo Building in Old Hall Street, a Ferry is breaking through the waves heading directly towards me, doing what a Ferry does best – providing one of the most spectacular journeys to work in the whole world.

These days, the Ferry as a 'work horse' is restricted to trips back and forth from MerseyTravel's Seacombe terminal to the Pier Head, including a free world-class river view, all for the price of a return ticket. Back in the 1970s, I used to take the Ferry to work every single day from Birkenhead to Liverpool, one of 7 million passengers a year at that time.

Of course, in the 1950s, the number was as high as 30 million. At this time, the ferry meant only one thing to me, a child's journey to a Wirral seaside resort that I could see every day from our street, high on Everton's famous ridge – the incredible New Brighton with its outdoor and indoor fairs that hypnotically called out to every kid on Merseyside. Who could resist that packed beach with its deckchairs and donkeys, or an Art Deco Lido with its giant open air swimming pool?

Again, I was proud to write a special piece for one of the Liverpool Echo's special nostalgia magazines: 'New Brighton – Our Days Out Remembered'.

I highlighted the fact that, these days, parents all over the world aspire to take their kids to places like Walt Disney World Florida or Universal Studios Los Angeles to give them the ultimate theme park experience.

These trips not only knock a hole in your bank balance as big as the Jumbo Jet you will fly in, but also test your patience and staying

Boarding the ferry in 1960

power to the absolute limit in the wake of several mind-numbing hours in an airport transit lounge. Eventually, you will jet across an ocean with the kids getting increasingly hyper by the hour before eventually meeting Mickey on the other side of the world.

Back in the Fifties, we journeyed to our local funfair paradise in a matter of minutes, sailing on a Mersey Ferry for the princely sum of a few old pennies, an incredible experience in its own right.

It was actually cheaper to sail to Seacombe and walk the length of the Promenade, giving you a few more precious coins to fulfil your fairground fantasies.

Of course, New Brighton had its own pier then, and thousands of Merseysiders would pile off boat after boat to stride straight into their very own magic kingdom, set out across a gently sloping hill on the river's edge that was crowned with a giant Ballroom, featuring a Tower that rocketed even higher than its world famous counterpart in Blackpool.

Can you remember the tingling sense of high excitement as the chains of the landing stage bridge rattled out their song of seaside welcome, dropping a drawbridge to paradise across the heaving decks of ferries like Royal Iris or the Royal Daffodil?

The crews desperately tried to hold us back

The Royal Iris sets sail in 1958

behind the brass marker lines that were inlaid into the decks. To step an inch over that line invited a crushing trip to the nearest hospital, and so we all took no chances.

We stood at least two inches back, urged by ferrymen in navy blue sweaters to hold our ground, like the runners and riders at the start of the Grand National. Bang! When that 12 foot high bridge hit the deck, it was as the equivalent of the tape going up at Aintree. We now all ran as if our lives depended on it, rushing up the narrow gangway with the fairground sights, sounds and smells urging us to turn our canter into a gallop.

There were now three optional decisions to make. Turn left and rush down the slipway onto the beach to set up camp for the day. This option had the added incentive of an early donkey ride or even a swim in the royal blue Mersey (sewage at no extra charge in those days before United Utilities decided it

might be a good idea to clean up the river and invite the fish back!).

Option two was to turn right along the Prom towards the spectacular outdoor swimming Lido, a giant pool where you could sunbathe for England on its terraces (it was always sunny and warm in those days, wasn't it?)

Option Three was a straight dash into the Fairground and Pleasure Gardens. It was usually parents to the deckchairs on the beach, kids into funfair paradise, a separation that would only be ended by the tempting lunchtime thought of Spam, egg or jam butties, washed down with a bottle of water!

I can still visualise the fairground. As you entered, the opportunity to catch a plastic duck on the end of a fishing line was your first temptation. The lads, of course, were instinctively drawn to the most spectacular ride in the park, just beyond and to the left, the giant Figure of 8 rollercoaster. Its wooden slats provided a rattling and terrifying thrill of a lifetime.

This also gave you a spectacular view of the Tower and Ballroom atop the hill, and the children's amusement park and miniature railway alongside the promenade below.

In previous decades, historic attractions at New Brighton had included the 1910 Aeroplane Ride, a roundabout featuring three large wooden planes that took to the air on the end of crane-like arms. Each plane could hold about six people.

The Caterpillar ride was introduced in the 1940s, circling up and down around a circular track, each unit attached and painted to resemble the body of a giant caterpillar. This ride sustained itself for generations.

The oldest roundabout in the fairground was said to be the 'Dobby Horses' from the 1800s which we called 'Bobby Horses', our very own fantasy Grand National.

Old photographs show a Big Wheel, a wooden structure just 30 feet high with about ten double seats. Of course, this would be overshadowed by a later version.

There were Go-Karts by the Boating Lake at the top end of the site, and by 1961 a Cable Car took people from the beach entrance to the upper reaches. I seem to recall two people stood up in each metal 'Car', a tight fit that added to the excitement and danger. There were side stalls all across the site.

My favourite was the Donkey Derby where you rolled a wooden ball towards a series of holes. Hitting those furthest away would gallop your horse quicker across the horizontal track, as the 'commentator' whipped up the excitement. I can remember winning a kite which I later flew on the beach for hours on end.

At the end of the day, exhausted, but

Crowds line the promenade at New Brighton

supremely happy, we would have to trek along the Prom to the Seacombe landing stage for the 'cheaper' ferry journey back across the river, having spent almost every penny in our riverside paradise.

We would then have to walk home from the Pier Head to our inner city Liverpool streets.

I felt privileged that at night I could see the coloured lights of New Brighton from where I lived on Everton's famous ridge, one of the highest vantage points in the city. I could also see the ferry boats from up there, plying their trade on a daily basis.

Those fairground lights would twinkle and send out a tantalising "come back soon" message that none of us could resist.

I also have a huge pride in the fact that the New Brighton resort was fashioned in the mind of one of my personal heroes, James Atherton, the merchant who in 1814 built the historic St. George's – the Cast Iron Church – where I would sing in the choir in the Fifties.

Atherton built many mansions in Everton, and his own stood to the left of the west gate of St. George's with his garden stretching down from Northumberland Terrace to Netherfield Road.

This gave him an uninterrupted view of the River Mersey at that time, and he was continually fascinated by a strip of land on the Wirral side that was known as 'Black Rock'.

In 1830, Atherton, in association with his son-in-law William Rowson, began negotiations with John Penkett, Lord of the Manor of Liscard, to purchase this land at the north-eastern end of the Township.

Effectively, his successful development of Everton represented a blueprint for his subsequent plans for New Brighton.

Atherton had proved to be an astute businessman with an eye for profit and he recognised the enormous seaside potential of 'Black Rock' both as a resort, and for the building of further smart mansions for the rich.

He also recognised that his own Everton mansion would soon be over-run by thousands of back to back terraced streets that were encroaching up the hill from the dock gates. This precipitated his move to New Brighton.

On 24th January 1832, William Rowson advanced a deposit of £200 to John Penkett to buy the 'New Brighton Estate'. The sum represented £100 each for himself and James Atherton.

This £200 would become the "deposit" for the seaside resort that would eventually capture the imagination of hundreds of thousands of Merseysiders and shape our childhood leisure days so magnificently, giving Liverpool families crucial respite from poverty and two World Wars.

James Atherton died in 1838. His dream would inspire us all for well over a century and we should thank him for the magic kingdom of New Brighton and a thousand childhood memories that we will never forget.

Sadly, New Brighton's ultimate demise as a major seaside attraction would be directly linked with the 1960s 'clearances' that destroyed districts like Everton and Scottie Road.

The new Wallasey Tunnel became the revised route to New Brighton. It seemed to be the beginning of the end for the Ferries as a genuinely viable transport option.

Thankfully, the Ferries have made something of a recovery now, as much a Merseyside tourist attraction to a worldwide visitor audience as the Liver Building, the Albert Dock or the Mathew Street Beatles quarter.

Mersey Travel have inspired a lifesaving Ferries revival.

All we need now is for the New Brighton Pier and Tower Ballroom to be rebuilt and everything will be right with the world once more!

An old well is discovered in Everton in 1963

CHAPTER 9

ROLL UP, ROLL UP, AND SEE THE BIGGEST RAT EVER CAUGHT IN A LIVERPOOL SEWER!

Local folklore tells of someone going to work one dark, misty morning and seeing a plague of rats migrating across the Dock Road

HAVING just revelled in my own memories of Merseyside's very own magic kingdom, Mrs. C. Lord of Liverpool 11 provided further memories of great days out "across the water". She recalled a sign in the famous New Brighton open air fairground that said:

"Come and see the biggest rodent caught in a Liverpool sewer."

The rat was actually a giant Coypu, a rodent found mainly in South America and Africa, but its size must have struck knowing looks and smiles from those visitors who would soon be heading back to Everton and Scottie Road. Ah, look. It's just a baby!

When I was growing up in Everton in the early 1950s, the large rats that came out to play in our narrow back entries clearly felt as much a part of the local community as you and me. We didn't invite them into our houses like loved friends and neighbours, but they often came to call anyway. No wonder our parents instinctively employed voracious cats to challenge the right to roam of these rodent visitors.

In my first 'Lost Tribe' book, I revealed how I arrived home with my parents one night and

Looking down on the famous Tate & Lyle factory

found a rat the size of a cat sitting in the middle of the parlour, apparently without a care in the world. It didn't seem over-bothered when my father grabbed the cast iron poker, probably because it was expecting a saucer of hot tea before retiring to Everton's deep and dark sewers.

All of this came back to me when I received a letter from John Pickavant whose father worked in a stable in Bute Street. John said: *"My dad fed and watered about eight horses twice a day. On Sundays, he would go to his allotment and leave me to water the horses in the afternoon. I once forgot, and when dad returned and asked if everything was okay, I said yes.*

"When it got dark, I got the keys and went to the stable. I walked up to the doors, opened them and switched on the lights.

"I was surrounded by rats and it seemed as if there were hundreds of them. They were running up the walls and across the floor into the hayloft above. I ran for my life, scared stiff and shaking.

"I knew I had to give those horses a drink, and eventually plucked up the courage to go back, but what a nightmare."

I'm inclined to give your story an X-certificate, John. But how would you have coped working on of those famous work places near the Liverpool Docks like Tate & Lyle's, Bibby's and Silcocks? The pungent, sharp, yet inviting aromas of the sugar, grain, and cattle food warehouses ensured that the resident rats outnumbered the workers a thousand to one?

I knew an amazing lady called Susannah Wright from Prince Edwin Street. She would tell me about her days working down near the docks where the rats were all on time and a half. Nothing frightened these women and, for a laugh, they would take the sandwiches out of a man's lunch box, and replace it with . . . yes, you've guessed it!

You can imagine the uproar, the expletives, and the roars of laughter, and that was only from the army of watching rats!

I always wondered what happened when all of those dockside warehouses and factories were demolished. I heard a bit of local folklore about someone going to work one dark, misty morning and seeing a plague of rats migrating across the Dock Road from a demolished warehouse to something a bit more substantial.

A few years later, we were migrating in our thousands in similar fashion as our houses and streets were pulled down around us and so I have some sympathy for our underground rodent neighbours.

And, just maybe, one of them took the ferry across the river to accept a very different role in a New Brighton fairground. No more grain, sugar, or cattle feed to eat, but what an accolade.

'The biggest rat ever to come out of a Liverpool sewer!'

Roll up, roll up – but get down off those chairs!

A view of Edinburgh Street and below, children play amid the debris on Buckingham Street

After the war, it was a time for having fun and enjoying ourselves, but sadly on a bomb site where previously there had been five streets packed with local families

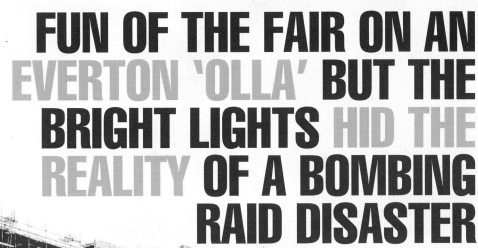

FUN OF THE FAIR ON AN EVERTON 'OLLA' BUT THE BRIGHT LIGHTS HID THE REALITY OF A BOMBING RAID DISASTER

Kids play under Abram Street as usual as the giant High Rise monoliths rise above them on Netherfield Road

IN the aftermath of the Second World War, the bulldozers rolled in and flattened the top half of Everton's Rose Vale, Anthony Street, Arkwright Street, Opie Street and Beatrice Street. 'Lost Tribe' reader Les Thompson recalled that they covered the whole area with black cinders and it became known as the 'top olla'. Les said:

"A man called Charlie Pepper organised a football team. He bought yellow shirts and they were known as the Canaries. They played against anyone who could get a team together.

"The football slowly disappeared and the 'top olla' went quiet, but not for long. One Christmas in the late 1940s, along came a fair, first at the Kirkdale Road end of Great Homer Street, but then at the top of Arkwright Street.

"For a number of years, it was really something to look forward to. I would walk up Dorrington Street in the dark, and as I turned the corner everything lit up. I can still hear the roar of the diesel engines driving the rides, with mams, dads and their children screaming on the 'Waltzer'.

"A man on a loud speaker would be calling the Bingo numbers, and nearby lads would be trying to 'Beat the Goalie'.

"But the sound that never left me was the music above the noise. After the war, it was time for having fun and enjoying ourselves, but sadly on a bomb site where previously there had been five streets packed with local families."

I must admit, Les, your memory rocked me to the core, because many of us look back on the old bomb sites – be they called the olla, the oller, or the debris – with huge affection.

These areas gave us our own football and cricket pitches. We would put coats or jumpers down for goal posts, or build wickets with half bricks.

We used these bomb sites for our street games and while we might have come home covered in muck and in need of a dip in the tin bath, they were the centre of our childhood universe at times.

On Netherfield Road North, between Melbourne Street where I lived and the

What a playground. Three boys make their own fun above these Netherfield Road high rise blocks

Victoria Settlement community centre, there was a debris area which we used as a sloping cricket pitch. It was totally devoid of grass.

My mother always used to tell me about the night the bottom of our street was devastated by Second World War bombing, probably a parachute mine, but I must admit, I never really thought too much about it in my childhood years as our cricket games unfolded. It was a play area in my mind.

However, a gentleman sent me a letter not too long ago in which he explained exactly what had happened to create that debris.

He recalled that during the War, as a young boy, he was taken up Netherfield Road from the Valley end by his father, only to be stopped by a police cordon at the bottom of Melbourne Street.

His father was allowed through and when he returned, looking shocked, it was clear that many people had been killed by a bombing raid, including members of his own family.

I knew exactly what those large Victorian houses looked like on Netherfield Road, with their steep steps up to the front door and with their large cellars below.

My close friend Graham Jennings lived in one on the side of Melbourne Street that escaped damage. All the properties on the other side of the street, right up to the towering walls of the Settlement, were destroyed.

Like Les Thompson, this made me think with mixed emotions about these bomb

Demolition squads at work after a German Luftwaffe raid on a street off 'Greaty' in 1941

sites. Our nostalgic 'debris' playgrounds were someone else's Second World War nightmare.

But we could do nothing about it as kids. In those post war years, we simply had to make the most of our limited inner city facilities and this included capitalising on all of those rough open spaces.

These days, Marie McGiveron is the Chief Executive of the Vauxhall Neighbourhood Council in Silvester Street, but this former City Councillor will tell you that the 'oller' she played on was her very own 'Garden of Eden' and one of the reasons why she has always tried to fight for her community in and around the famous Scotland Road.

This once vibrant thoroughfare has suffered many body blows since the City Council's slum clearance and development programme unfolded from the start of the 1960s.

But of all the projects that destroyed the heart of Scottie, perhaps the most catastrophic blow was the building of the Kingsway Mersey Tunnel which was opened by the Queen in June 1971.

Its sweeping approach road would not only turn the southern end of Scottie into a huge no-man's land, but also take with it some famous streets including the likes of Cazneau Street which was once linked with Scotland Road and bordered the western side of the former open air market.

This giant hole in the ground now encompassed what would become the Kingsway Industrial Park as well as the circling approach route to the Wallasey Tunnel entrance.

Older Liverpudlians still use the phrase going 'over the water' when talking about a trip to the Wirral. This was the second 'under the water' road route, following on from the construction of the first Mersey road tunnel (Queensway) in 1934.

In some respects, Scottie Road has simply never recovered from this body blow.

Another major threat to the district emerged when a plan was unveiled to build a major inner city ring road in 1975 that would have effectively put a motorway right through the community, beginning at where Vauxhall Road / Leeds Street now stands.

Marie recalls how this inspired the 'Homes Not Roads' campaign that won huge support in the Vauxhall Road, Scotland Road and Everton areas. She said:

"We blocked all the traffic in the city with our demonstrations. The former Merseyside County Council hated us at the time. We even got thrown out of the Town Hall, but it highlighted the fighting spirit of the people in our communities and the road was never built.

"We also had the rent strike in the 1970s. It was about the introduction of the Housing Finance Act. Everyone paid the same rent at that time, but the new plan would bring in different levels.

"The Labour Party in Liverpool said they would never introduce it. Then they did and it led to citywide action around 1972.

"Everyone in the community started withholding part of the increase. The residents 'Over the Bridge' (at the bottom of Hopwood and Boundary Streets) went on a full rent strike. We even put up tenants' candidates against local councillors as we challenged other things because no one was questioning the upheaval felt within the area at that time.

"For instance, the new Mersey Tunnel and its massive approach roads that had such a massive impact on Scotland Road should have been in the south end of the city, but the Council didn't take that option because they felt there would be more opposition down there.

"However, we soon became much more organised as a community as we came together to try and secure grants for local schemes. There is no way they would try to walk all over us today with something as impacting as a major ring road through our community.

"In the Seventies this area was the most deprived in the country. We remain in the top 1% for deprivation, something that has been clearly identified by the City Council.

"Unless we start at the bottom with an

absolute commitment to follow all the way through, things won't change.

"Physically, the area has improved 200% with lots of semi detached houses with gardens when it was once dominated by High Rise and poor housing, but the underlying problems around health and unemployment remain. These issues link together and if you don't sort one out, it affects the other.

"The one constant is that the people of the area have always been very special.

"When I was younger, things didn't seem so horrific because it was all we knew. We used to play on the 'oller' or the 'debris' – mostly caused by Second World War German bombing.
When I was a kid and learning about Adam and Eve, these desolate areas became my Garden of Eden."

It's hard to explain to people now how such basic and rough pieces of land, devoid of grass and trees, could become such evocative playgrounds for the kids of the inner cities, but they did. Marie's 'Garden of Eden' tag may seem to romanticise what was basically a muck, brick and boulder strewn environment, but if you lived there, you will know exactly what she is talking about. Kids could lose themselves in their street games and rituals as the area desperately tried to recover from the devastation of the War.

Sadly, the clearance bulldozers would finish off the job that was started by enemy bombers and Scotland Road would be left just a shadow of its previous majestic self, although the people have never stopped fighting for their community rights, inspired by groups like the Vauxhall Neighbourhood Council and the Eldonians who I talk to in more detail later in this book.

IMAGINE PUTTING YOUR CHILDREN ON AN EVACUATION TRAIN WITH NO IDEA WHEN YOU MIGHT SEE THEM AGAIN

The fear of not knowing what every day might bring was a constant worry for all war youngsters

I'VE been continually inspired, entertained and amused reading the letters sent to me by the 'Lost Tribe of Everton & Scottie Road', but every now and then a particular subject strikes a much deeper chord in relation to those dark days of the Second World War.

I was born in the immediate aftermath of the hostilities when rationing remained part and parcel of every family's routine and when the mantra was still make and mend. I've highlighted how, as kids, we played on the old debris sites, but looked on them as functional playgrounds rather than areas of bombing devastation.

Nevertheless, we knew life had been incredibly tough for people all over the city during the war, especially the kids who had to deal day and night with the terror of high explosive bombs, incendiary devices and the lethal parachute mines.

CHAPTER 11

Young children were separated from their parents for long periods. The smiles hide the fear, pain and trepidation of these evacuation exercises

Evacuees wait in a schoolroom for the arrival of their 'foster parents' in September 1939

Youngsters had to fend for themselves and adopt an instinctive survival mode without the fathers who were at war and the mothers who were encouraged to evacuate their children. Imagine what it would be like now to hand over a vulnerable five-year-old at a railway station with no understanding of where he or she was going, or who might be looking after them?

William Timson, who now lives near Wigan, was typical of the evacuation kids. He was born in Arkwright Street in Everton, an area devastated by the blitz bombing of May 1941. He was five when his mother reluctantly decided to send him and his sister to Pentir, near Bangor, where they lived with the family of a local headmaster.

"He was very strict," recalled William, "but we were not mistreated in any way. However,

we had to learn Welsh. We also had to carry our gas masks with us at all times, for school and church. I'm not sure how long we were away, but when we returned to Liverpool and Salisbury Street School, we were talking with Welsh accents and the other kids made fun of us."

William's father was then posted by the Royal Artillery to Walney Island, Barrow-in-Furness, and the family moved with him, yet another upheaval for the youngsters. The Timsons sold all of their furniture to neighbours in Arkwright Street. However, within days they heard that their old street had been heavily bombed and that amongst the people killed were the friends who had bought their furniture.

This fear of not knowing what every day might bring was a constant worry for all war youngsters. Incredibly, having had one spell

Evacuated young boys put on a brave face while a young girl (below) takes solace from her prized dolly

of evacuation during the war, William was sent away again, this time with a cousin. They spent two years in Wales at Colomendy Camp near Loggerheads between 1944 and 1946.

I'm not sure what would have been worse, staying in the city with your family in those war days with all the dangers that this posed, or being separated for such long periods from those you loved and trusted.

Either option must have been a nightmare. I have every respect for those who came through it without any of the counselling and support available today. Everybody just got on with it thanks to the powerful neighbourhood spirit that acted like a comfort blanket around the shoulders of people who found themselves in need of moral and physical help.

Sir Henry Morton Stanley, who resided in Everton before his famous trip to Africa, where he found Dr. Livingstone

CHAPTER 12

AFRICAN EXPLORERS AND A HOUSE IN 'ROSSY' EVERTON

The knighthood of Sir Henry Morton Stanley highlighted the remarkable turn around in his fortunes from his low key days living in Everton

EVERTON has a famous connection with Sir Henry Morton Stanley, the well known explorer, as any old residents of Roscommon Street will tell you.

An inscribed brass plate used to take pride of place on the wall of a house in the street, declaring that the Welsh-born American journalist had slept there before he sailed to Africa in 1871, to find the legendary Scottish missionary and fellow explorer Dr. David Livingstone who had lost contact with the outside world for six years.

On finding Livingstone, Stanley, uttered the famous words:

"Dr. Livingstone I presume?"

Mrs E. Morris from Liverpool 4 told me: *"At one point, the plaque mentioned was above the door of the old Homeopathy Hospital at the bottom of Roscommon Street, on the right hand side coming up from Great Homer Street."*

Joan Murray from Liverpool 13 has actually written a local history booklet which touches on the subject.

She explains: *"Stanley is probably more famous for finding Livingstone than for his journalistic writings. He lived with an uncle*

Sir Paul McCartney's family lived in the Sir Thomas White Gardens tenements, pictured here in 1938

named Tom Morris at 22 Roscommon Street. Stanley started work at a haberdashery shop in London Road, then as a butcher in a shop near to the Liverpool docks.

"Eventually he sailed for America as a cabin boy, which is where he took up residence before becoming a newspaper journalist."

Stanley came from a humble background. He was born John Rowlands in Denbigh in 1841. He changed his name in America and his ultimate knighthood highlighted the remarkable turn-around in his fortunes from his low key days living in Everton.

Everton can boast many famous former residents, not least another knight – Sir Paul McCartney. As a small boy, Macca lived in the Sir Thomas White Gardens tenements in Everton which stood at the top of our street. Doris Dewhurst (nee Shelley) contacted me to say: *"The famous Beatle's mother was a midwife and she looked after my mother when* she was expecting my younger sister Jackie. We were in the first block of flats as you came into 'Tommy Whites' from Beacon Lane. The blocks all looked in on inner squares where the kids played football and cricket. We also had big bonfires in the squares on Guy Fawkes Night (November 5) and kept these going all night."

Of course, Macca would write about 'Penny Lane', and even the 'Mull of Kintyre'. Ringo penned a song entitled 'Liverpool 8' about his boyhood home with the words:

Liverpool I left you,
Said 'goodbye' to Madryn Street
I always followed my heart
And I never missed a beat
Destiny was calling, I just couldn't stick around
Liverpool I left you, but I never let you down

Come on Paul, I'm sure you can come up with something on 'Tommy Whites'!

A small plaque in Roscommon Street in 1970, records the former residence of Sir Henry Morton Stanley. Hunt and St. John were more modern heroes

Pictured in 1988, Winnie Boyle, was one of the oldest tenants in Paddy's Market

CHAPTER 13

GRANNIES, NINS, NANS AND GRANDMAS – MATRIARCHS OF OUR FAMOUS STREETS

Pink fleece-lined bloomers, and three petticoats tied with tape around the waist, with a 'pocket' on top

THE districts of Everton and Scottie Road, in tandem with all the old inner city districts, had some remarkable characters.

June Woodall provided a wonderful visual image of her grandmother that we will all relate to. She said:

"One of my early memories is of my grandmother getting dressed in the morning. Over the top of pink fleece-lined bloomers, she wore three petticoats tied with tape around her waist. On top of that she had a 'pocket' – similar to what decorators have these days to keep their bits and pieces in. The 'pocket' was striped blue and white, and in it she kept her purse and her insurance books. Her dress came on top of all of this, finished off with black woollen stockings and black shoes, whatever the weather."

June added: *"My grandmother liked a bet on the horses, and I would take it to a bookie in Reading Street, Kirkdale. These were the days before Betting Shops (when street betting was actually illegal). The bookie's house was on the first landing. It was a no-go area and I was only ten years of age, so I would run there and back as fast as I could."*

Many people will have similar memories, not least from the 1950s and earlier.

June continued: *"Every night my grandmother would go down to the 'The Pansy' pub on Stanley Road for her supper beer, as she called it. My cousin Betty and I would walk her across and put her in her favourite seat where she would wait for her friend 'Yocky' to join her.*

"Grandmother always had salt fish hanging up in the kitchen and she would use the fish to slap us with. Happy days!"

What a tremendous picture you paint, June, and I love the story about salt fish. It's still my 88-year-old father's favourite, and when he cooks it, the whole block where he lives knows what's for tea. I'm sure many other people have been told: *"Behave or I'll slap you with a salt fish."*

The women of the inner cities were all powerful matriarchs, loved and adored by their big families. These ladies deserve our absolute respect. Incredibly, the newspaper headlines these days are full of shocking stories regarding the way many senior citizens are being treated in hospitals and nursing homes around the country.

I was hugely encouraged by a letter from Kath Binnion. She told me about her next door neighbour who died at the age of 103.

Kath said:

"She was absolutely wonderful. She always insisted on having her hair and nails done. She would have prunes for breakfast and white fish for lunch. She was put into a home at 88. Earlier in her life she had been a nanny to two young boys. They visited her at the Home and realised how unhappy she was.

"They decided to bring her home to her own bungalow and continued to care for her. One of those 'boys', Brian, is now turned 85 himself!

"Brian can now enjoy his own life after giving so much to make an old lady happy. When we think of the old days, we cared for our loved ones the best way we could and the chair old granny sat in was always treasured."

Thanks for that uplifting story, Kath. You clearly lost a lovely neighbour and they can be few and far between in a world in which community togetherness of any description is not always apparent. We certainly take everything for granted these days, but Lost Tribe readers continue to remind me of a time when things were very different.

June Woodall said: *"At the outbreak of World War 2, many of the children were evacuated along with their teachers. Those who didn't go often had no schools to attend because the Council had closed them.*

"Many ordinary women let off a front room or parlour to the few teachers and pupils left and that's where they held their lessons. My two aunties let rooms out. When the bombing stopped quite a few evacuees came back and the schools started to open up again."

Large families were commonplace, as shown by this photo of a gathering, taken at the back of Fox Street

June added: *"Because many young men and women were called up to the Services, we were taught by middle aged and often quite elderly women. I've got to hand it to them. They certainly knew how to teach and to impose discipline. I had the finest education one could wish for and it has stayed with me to this day."*

Margaret Boden has vivid memories relating to the big families of the day. She recalls:

"My mum always seemed to be having babies. When I was about ten, my sister and I would be sent in the dead of night to fetch the midwife in Everton Valley who would tell us to carry the gas and air bottles back to the house, saying 'I'll be up soon.'

"We used to carry this heavy case together, but never looked inside. It must have been dangerous for kids to be entrusted with something like that. It would never happen today.

"If anything needed moving, it was always the big kids who would be sent. My cousin Tommy Gollock and I once pushed a handcart with a piano on top from Bootle to Everton, including negotiating the steep Everton Valley.

"Health and safety also didn't exist in the Donaldson Street wash house. You had to be 15 to go in, but mum would dress me up in wellies and put a turban on my head to make me look older. I would be kept off school.

"Our mothers should not have let it happen, but that was life then and it had to be done."

Nothing kept down the powerful matriarchs of Everton,
even when the mains water was cut off during demolition

Everton's famous ridge was 'Hollywood' and a green paradise overlooking the city for the rich merchants who built their grand villas. This is from a litho by C. Towne. Below left, Islington Market in 1843 and right, St. George's Church, with its original decorative roof fineals that were removed for safety reasons

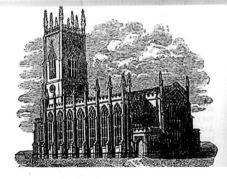

THE LADY OF THE MANOR WHO SOLD HALF OF EVERTON FOR THE PRINCELY SUM OF JUST £115

In the eighteenth century you could have bought Everton in its entirety for £230!

EVERTON once had some of the most sought after addresses in the city. The district's upper slopes – which I have described as Merseyside's very own 'Hollywood' – were dotted with expensive villas and mansions in the 19th Century.

Many of these were built by James Atherton, the inspirational figure behind the completion of St. George's – the 'Iron Church' – which opened its doors in 1814.

These days there is very little to see of these impressive properties which is why the district's only two remaining terraces of any note, one on Shaw Street and the other on Everton Road, should be protected at all costs. Only the façade remains of the Shaw Street Terrace with the properties behind completely rebuilt, but it continues to stand as a massively important local landmark.

Shaw Street was laid out by Liverpool councillor Thomas Shaw in 1828 with the first house built the following year. Through marriage, Shaw's father had inherited the extensive Everton estate of the famous Halsall family.

The Halsalls links with Everton stretch back

Everton Terrace in 1867 (by W. Herdman) with the Collegiate in the distance

to 1667 when William Halsall is recorded as owning up to 55 statute acres. In 1716 Lady Ashburnham, Lady of the Manor of Everton, as the only surviving daughter and heiress of William, Earl of Derby, dispensed with 245 statute acres of unenclosed land in Everton, called the Breck (Breck Road).

This area was split into three divisions of the Manor known as Whitefields (marked by Whitefield Road), Netherfields (Netherfield Road), and Hangfields (the modern district of Anfield). Henry Halsall, a descendant of William Halsall, secured 25 acres as his share, adding these to the family property which he had inherited. Lady Ashburnham is said to have secured the princely sum of £115 for her 245 acres which made up nearly the half of Everton!

This suggests you could have bought Everton in its entirety at that time for £230!

The Halsall family mansion with its substantial gardens and grounds stood on Everton Road.

The site would become Lloyd Street (now Lloyd Close), Aubrey Street (now Aubrey Close), and Spencer Street, amongst others. The Everton Village Cross was directly opposite the Halsalls' front drive.

In 1780 the last of the male Halsalls on Everton Road died childless and his widow inherited everything.

The highly respected Shaw family were watching all of this unfold. James Shaw had come from Newton-le-Willows in the early 18th century, setting up a Dale Street business with his brothers. There was nothing much beyond Dale Street at that time other than the wild heath which extended up the hill into Everton.

Samuel Shaw recognised the opportunities within this heathland and erected an extensive pottery on the sloping ground, soon known as Shaw's Brow, now William Brown Street. His son Thomas would become Liverpool's Mayor in 1747.

Brow Side butchers of James Haughton in 1859 (by W. Herdman)

The Shaws were becoming increasingly influential and a prominent member of the family, John Shaw, caught the eye of Mr. Halsall's widow and they were married. John survived his wife and inherited all of the Halsall estates in Everton, which included the fields from the end of Netherfield Road South to the top of Islington.

This made him the most important landowner in the district, and he was known as 'Squire Shaw'. In 1800, he became the second Shaw to be invested as Mayor of Liverpool which brings this story full circle.

It was his son, Thomas Shaw, who cut a new road across these fields to connect Netherfield Road South and Moss Street.

You will not be surprised that he called it Shaw Street.

It was opened in 1829 and the following year St. Augustine's Church, with its unusually shaped tower, was erected. This would soon stand alongside the prestigious College (later the Collegiate School) which was opened in 1843. Shaw clearly had big ideas for his new street and his plan was to preserve the whole district for large houses, occupied by Liverpool's richest merchants.

However, this scheme would be completely undermined by the building of rows of small houses in Canterbury Street and Salisbury Street intended for the growing working class population of Everton. Similar streets were now encroaching on the mansions and villas on all sides of the district.

St. Francis Xavier's Church opened its doors in 1848 opposite the Collegiate to ultimately become the biggest Roman Catholic Parish in the country.

Sadly, the distinctive St. Augustine's was destroyed during the May Blitz of 1941.

Shaw's legacy is a still famous thoroughfare with a rich history, not least on the medical and dentistry side. An important example of this will unfold in the next chapter.

The famous Shaw Street terrace in 1958

REMARKABLE STORY OF 55 SHAW STREET – AND THE MEN WHOSE MEDICAL EXPERTISE PROVED INSPIRATIONAL

In the 1830s and 1840s the majority of Liverpool's leading doctors and dentists lived in an area which encompassed Everton's Shaw Street, St. Anne Street and Islington

HAVING just given you an insight into the importance of Shaw Street, it is fascinating to follow the history of one specific house, number 55.

As a kid, I remember Shaw Street as the last place I wanted to visit, but only because my dentist was there. These were the days when an anaesthetic mask would be thrust over your face to send you into a nether world of strange dreams. On one occasion, having been 'put under', I was dreaming that I was playing in a football match and that I had been injured and knocked unconscious.

I could sense a mild slap across the face and a distant voice urging: *"Come on Kenny, you're fine. Wake up now."*

Of course, I was not wearing my football boots when the lights eventually came on.

I was lying back in that dentist's chair with my mother standing by with a large scarf that I used to cover my mouth on the long walk home along Shaw Street and Netherfield Road to the safety of 8 Melbourne Street.

The only consolation was that the tooth fairy would gain entrance to my bedroom that night. No doubt she fluttered down the chimney (every room in the house had a fireplace) before leaving the traditional shiny sixpence under my pillow. I was pretty much considering having all of my teeth out at that point, obviously with separate appointments for every extraction.

I'd worked out that my remaining teeth were worth at least fifteen 'bob' (75p in modern money) and understood all too well that a boy from Everton could do a hell of a lot with such a massive windfall. Remember, I just told you that a famous lady once sold half the district for £115!

But back to Shaw Street, the home of dentists and some excellent doctors as well.

Amongst these was the late Dr. William 'Bill' Mackean whose family first occupied the aforementioned number 55 in 1921. The Mackeans would still be serving the district over 40 years later.

Local residents in need of medical care and attention had long been making a beeline to 55 Shaw Street. In 1868, the property was the home of Dr. Ben Townson and his wife Mary.

While the terrace looked uniform in its appearance, the houses were all individually designed. Number 55 had three spacious entertaining rooms with fine mahogany doors and large sash windows.

The drawing-room windows, with their wrought iron balconies, looked down on a small park (still there today).

These properties were in stark contrast to those in the surrounding streets, tiny and erected with the minimum of fuss for the working class of the district.

The Townsons were Quakers and they insisted that all members of the family, together with the servants and anyone visiting the house, should meet and pray together at breakfast before starting their daily routine.

Ben Townson observed total abstinence from alcohol which was still being used by many doctors at that time as an indispensable medical treatment.

Ben was probably the first Liverpool practitioner to stand alone against the medical opinion of his day and attempt the treatment

of acute disease without the aid of alcohol.

He also condemned smoking, a brave stance in an era when it was a national pastime for men, seen by many as actually being a healthy thing to do.

How do I know this? Well, I was fortunate to meet the engaging Dr. Bill Mackean, who was kind enough to provide me with a copy of the fascinating address he gave to the Liverpool Medical Institution as its President on 8 October 1992.

The subject matter was 'The Square Mile' and highlighted the fact that, in the 1830s and 1840s before the pre-eminence of Rodney Street, the majority of Liverpool's leading doctors and dentists lived in an area which encompassed Everton's Shaw Street, St. Anne Street, and Islington.

One of these was Ben Townson, and Bill Mackean was fascinated by their mutual link with 55 Shaw Street.

Townson was ahead of his time in the early and mid-nineteenth century when Liverpool had 138,244 people per square mile, the highest population density outside of London (243,000).

Of course, taken in isolation, the Everton and Scotland Road districts had a population density the equivalent of 460,000 people per square mile. Here, 8,000 residents were so crowded together there was a living space of little over 9 feet by 6 feet for each person.

The spread of disease and infection was rife in these inner city districts and men like Townson worked side by side with the inspirational Dr. William Henry Duncan, the Medical Officer of Health for Liverpool, to help the working class in places like Everton.

Townson died in 1886 and his funeral at Anfield Cemetery was attended by various temperance societies, a detachment of postmen in uniform (he had been the Post Office doctor for 42 years), and perhaps most

Residents were crowded together and the spread of disease and infection was rife

touchingly the 'barefooted poor of Everton' whose plight he had always referred to in his morning prayers.

Townson had handed over his Shaw Street practice to his wife's nephew, John Herbert Thorp, who carried on the temperance tradition.

As a journalist, newspaperman and former Everton boy, I have a lot of admiration for Dr. Thorp who was Honorary Physician to the Newsboys' Home, and the Home for Friendless Boys in Everton Road. He was also very close to the old Industrial School on Everton Terrace.

Dr. Thorp kept the medical traditions of 55 Shaw Street going for a further 35 years before selling the practice to a 51-year-old Scot, J. Findlay Stevenson, who set up the Liverpool Medical, Dental and Pharmaceutical Agency at the address in 1921.

But rather than act as a clearing house for practices, he now amalgamated five into one, including Dr. Thorp's, and it was at this juncture that the Mackean family arrived on the scene to make a huge impact on the district which they now adopted as their own.

Dr. Robert Mackintosh Mackean, Bill Mackean's father, was working in an Ayrshire mining village when he spotted an advert for the enlarged Shaw Street practice.

The challenge excited him and he invested £3,700 in the opportunity, a significant amount of money at that time. More to the point, he wanted to invest his time and energy into improving the lot of Everton's working class whom he didn't just serve, but thoroughly respected.

When Robert Mackean first arrived at 55 Shaw Street, it was the custom for patients to be sent down the steps in front of the house to wait in the basement in a large room with a stone floor.

They would then wait to be called up to the consulting room which was at the back of the house on the ground floor.

They left by the same route, therefore avoiding using the hall. Dr. Robert Mackean felt this was demeaning, insisting the patients now used the front door, while using the spacious middle dining room as a waiting area. This overlooked the courtyard, a much brighter proposition than waiting in a dark and gloomy basement.

Robert Mackean was the first doctor in Everton to have a car, and he employed a uniformed 14-year-old boy to look after it when he made his house calls up and down the surrounding steep streets.

The vehicle was like a magnet to the local lads who would circle round to get a closer view.

Back at the surgery, the other interesting thing was that practice medicines were always dispensed by the doctor, not a separate chemist, and so there was a room behind the consulting area with rows of shelves.

Scales were used to weigh powders, with measuring vessels for the liquid medicines. Bottles would be wrapped neatly in green paper for collection by the patients later in the day.

The family immersed themselves in the day to day life of Everton and in July, 1928, a baby would now be born at 55 Shaw Street – christened William Mackintosh Mackean.

It was almost inevitable that this infant would follow in his father's medical footsteps to serve the future generations of Everton, Walton, Anfield and Kirkdale.

Sefton General Hospital; right, Dr. William Mackean

CHAPTER 16

EVERTON DOCTOR WHO DROVE A MORRIS 8 DOWN A SEFTON GENERAL HOSPITAL CORRIDOR

Bill Mackean would earn the respect of the Everton community he served in the ensuing decades

YOUNG William Mackean was not born with the prefix Dr. before his name, but it was almost a given that he would carry on the work of his father.

Bill was a pupil at Liverpool College from 1936 to 1945 and studied medicine at Liverpool University from 1945.

He qualified in 1951, and the new Dr. Mackean became a house physician to Dr. Arnold Grunberg at St. Catherine's Hospital, and a house surgeon to Mr. James Cosbie Ross, Bill Beattie and Jimmy Gow at Sefton General Hospital.

Whilst working as a Casualty Officer at Sefton General Hospital in 1953, Bill Mackean gained some notoriety when he drove a 1932 Morris 8 down a corridor on Christmas Day with a number of nurses hitching a ride!

They disappeared when Dr. Mackean was confronted by the irate Matron.

In 1953 he started his National Service in the Royal Navy, serving aboard HMS Loch Quoich in the Indian Ocean where, within a short space of time, he had performed two appendicectomies in very difficult conditions.

In fact, there was no ether to use as one of

A 1932 Morris 8, like the one driven down a corridor of Sefton General Hospital by Dr. Bill Mackean

the crew had used it all up to clean his brass buttons!

Dr. Mackean remained in the Naval Reserve after completing his service and reached the rank of Surgeon Commander. He was awarded a Reserve Decoration in 1968.

After National Service, Bill went on a refresher course and was intending to serve his GP 'apprenticeship' with his father in Shaw Street. However, Dr. Robert Mackean was involved in a car accident while on duty and Bill was thrust into the front line as solo GP in the practice for five months with no previous experience.

Having worked alone since 1921, his father now took the opportunity to hand all of the 'on-call' work to his son and that fierce régime existed for seven years until the Deputising Service was formed in 1962.

Bill Mackean, who married Nan Ferris from Kent in 1958, would earn the respect of the Everton community he served in the ensuing decades. His story is typical of many of his colleagues who practised, and still practise in the area today.

I came across Bill when he became terminally ill during 2010. He had been given a copy of the 'Lost Tribe of Everton & Scottie Road' for his birthday and my book helped inspire memories of his working life in the district. He asked to see me and I travelled out to his house in Mossley Hill where his knowledge, humour and courage inspired me to write about 55 Shaw Street in this follow-up publication.

Sadly, Bill passed away on 2 November, 2010, within a short time of our meeting, but I felt as if I knew him well and was delighted when I heard that his five children – Susie, Lizzie, William, Robert, and John, plus friends

Taken during the 1980s, this photograph shows Bill Mackean finishing a half-marathon in Knowsley

and relatives – were running as Team Mackean in the 2011 Liverpool Marathon to remember him.

The day before the race, they asked if I would give them a short tour of Everton and we met outside 55 Shaw Street where we were also joined by Nan Mackean and Bill's grandchildren Zoe, Ruby, Esme, Tom, Lydia, Rachel and William.

We knocked on the door of what had been the doctor's surgery, now transformed into a series of residential flats, and it says everything about the incredibly warm nature of the people of the district, that we were welcomed inside to enable the Mackeans to spend a few treasured minutes remembering their father and everything that had unfolded there.

The following day every member of Team Mackean finished the marathon to complete their charity aims and raise £10,000 for the Marie Curie cancer charity.

Bill, who had run seven marathons himself, would have been proud of them, just like he was fiercely proud of the district both he and his father had jointly served with such distinction for over 40 years.

Wardens had to dig people out of heavily bombed properties

CHAPTER 17

SAVED FROM A MILL ROAD BOMBING NIGHTMARE BY A MOTHER'S INSTINCT

Over 4,000 were killed in the Blitz, as high explosives, incendiary bombs and parachute mines rained down on the city

AS the Liverpool Echo marked the 70th anniversary of Liverpool's 1941 May Blitz with a series of special articles, one of the stories that struck home with Nicola Kuypers from Wirral related to the dreadful bombing of Mill Road Hospital in Everton.

Nicola wrote to me on behalf of Josephine Sacker, explaining:

"Josephine was born at Mill Road on 9 April, 1941, which was the month before the Blitz. Due to the fact that she was born by Caesarean, she was required to stay in hospital for one month.

"However, her mother discharged herself and baby Josie the day before the hospital was bombed on 3 May, 1941. The bomb came through the window of the maternity ward where she had been staying and where many mothers, babies and nurses sadly lost their lives."

Josephine went on to have four children and 14 grandchildren of her own and while she has clearly had a very full and happy life, she can never forget what might have happened if her mother had not taken that fateful step to discharge them the day before the Mill Road disaster.

Fire watchers in training at an Everton ARP (Air Raid Precautions) School behind Everton Terrace Police Station. Anne Fowler's Women's Home is in the background

I have received many memories from individuals and families who were caught up in the Mersey Blitz devastation.

Mrs. T. Milburn from Seaforth recalled a remarkable escape at her family's former house at the end of Gray Street, off Knowsley Road, Bootle. She explained:

"Our front door faced the side wall of the Queen's pub. When the war started in 1939, I was just seven years old and my sister was three.

"My sister and I were asleep on the sofa when my mum came into the room. She sat by us and also fell asleep. A bomb crashed into the house and we were only saved because the sofa somehow turned over and covered us like a tent. The Air Raid Wardens came and got us out in the morning and we were saved because of that sofa. We were taken to recover at the nearby Peel Road Church Hall."

In May, 2011, I sat in a packed Liverpool Cathedral as the sound of a World War Two air raid siren signalled the start of a special service to commemorate the May Blitz anniversary.

As we listened to recordings of explosions overhead, it was clear just how frightening it must have been for the population of Merseyside. Over 4,000 were killed as high explosives, incendiary bombs and parachute mines rained down on a city whose response was to become even more defiant by the day.

James Davies, who now lives in Netherton, would later tell me:

"I was only nine when war broke out. By day my father, Edward Henry Davies, worked as a refuse collector for Bootle Corporation. By night he was an Air Raid Warden. My mother would be left with five young children, wondering if he would come home the following morning.

"I can remember my mother telling us about dad rescuing people from their bombed houses, or helping to recover the bodies of the dead. I can still picture myself standing on the back step of our house in William Morris Avenue, Bootle, watching dog fights in the sky and, on one occasion, seeing a parachutist falling from a stricken plane.

"Much has been said about the terrific effort made by all the emergency services at that time, but I don't feel the Air Raid Wardens got the credit they deserved."

Les Thompson from Liverpool 12 also highlighted the debt we owe to the ARPs. Les recalled the raid that devastated five streets off Netherfield Road, close to where I would eventually be brought up in Everton. Les lived in Russell Square. He said:

"Rose Vale, Anthony Street, Arkwright Street, Opie Street and Beatrice Street were all hit. I was only about four. If the bombs had landed 500 yards further down, we would have got it.

"The next morning, mam got us ready. As we started to walk up Arkwright Street, we were covered in a choking thick grey and brown dust. We had to turn back.

"Later we got some bad news. My Nan and her two children, Audrey and Wilf, were trapped

in a cellar in Anthony Street. My grandad was never found. He was an Air Raid Warden. Eventually they rescued Nan and the others through a coal grid.

"Nan later revealed that grandad had told them to go into the cellar because he knew it was going to be a night of heavy bombing. Nan wanted him to stay, but he told them he had to do his duty as an ARP.

"As I was putting this memory together, I heard that Aunty Audrey had died. She was 88 on May 3rd and died on May 4th, exactly 70 years to the week that she was trapped in the cellar. She must have had her 18th birthday down there that terrible night."

I received many Blitz stories, but one 'great escape' really inspired me. Joyce Phillips (nee McMurray) was just six when she went with her parents into the cellar of Walton Lane School to take shelter with the caretaker and his family. They were joined by a lady carrying her one month old baby.

Joyce recalled:
"It was a very bad night with bombs going off all around. The school was hit hard and in the cellar we could feel the walls falling down, the dust, the rumbling and the darkness. Then water appeared on the floor. The water main had burst. We were trapped and did not know how to get out.

"My dad started moving bricks with his bare hands and managed to make a hole in the rubble. We could hear the Air Raid Wardens outside and they managed to drag us out. My dad stayed behind and positioned his body to stop the bricks falling down.

"He cradled the baby in his arms to protect her. She was covered with dust and her shawl was blackened.

"Dad was taken to hospital with head injuries. He suffered with headaches for the rest of his life. After emerging from underground, we found our house had been badly damaged. We stood in Bodley Street and watched the school burn. Seventy years later I can still remember the smell of that night."

Of course, we should never forget the Merseyside soldiers who fought in campaigns all over the world (and who still do us proud in modern theatres of war). Rose Davie sent me a poem written by a soldier just before the battle of El Alamain, fought in the deserts of North Africa in 1942.

Rose's husband Jim was in the RAF. Soldiers used the word 'Doover' as slang for a slit trench, covered with corrugated iron, and then sand. They would climb in so they could not be seen by the Germans, and peer out through the narrow slit. I have shortened the poem, but it still paints a vivid picture.

MY DOOVER IN THE BLUE

It's a haven, home from home
My doover in the blue
The only land I've ever owned
My block with desert view

I built it to a pattern
That every squaddie knows
There is no room for comfort
Just safety and repose

It's nothing much to look at
That's where the beauty lies
For the Jerry 'bird' can't see me
When over me he flies

The Stukas give no warning
As they dive from sun and cloud
As I tie myself into a knot
And curse with fear aloud

The doover shakes and trembles
The walls come caving in
But, when the blitz is over
I pat them with a grin

I share my hole with spiders
A scorpion, a snake or two
But still, I love my dug-out
My doover in the blue

It would take more than a trip to B & Q to find a solution for this huge crack in an old Everton house

CHAPTER 18

STAR GAZING
THROUGH A CRACK
IN A 'SCOTCH
HOUSE' WALL

Rats at home and then 'rats' in the ring, as the bad boys of wrestling stirred up the Stadium crowd

JAMES MAHER from Liverpool 14 provided a fascinating insight into the old 'Scotch Houses' that were once an integral part of heartland Everton and Scottie Road.

James described in vivid detail the desperate conditions people had to put up with.

Once again, I marvel at how the residents of our inner city streets still manage to look back with inspirational memories of the people and the communities who lived in these areas. James told me:

"Between 1942 and 1945 I lived at 17 Sim Street, which was off Langsdale Street, Everton. The street is now occupied by new properties.

"We lived in the 'Scotch Houses' which were one up, one down, or one on top of the other. Each had a small living room, one bedroom, a kitchen and an outside toilet. We lived on top of a family called the 'Mees'.

"The kitchen, bedroom, toilet and slate stairs going up into the house had no light. The only light came from a living room gas mantle. I remember there was a big wide crack in the wall, caused by Second World War bombing,

through which you could see the sky. It was our own 'built-in ventilation!'

"In the winter the house was freezing, but it didn't stop us going into the tin bath in front of the open fire. The next street up was Page Street with the 'Great Eastern' pub on the corner. At the top of Sim Street was Johnny Nuttall's Sweet Shop. He only sold Swizzels (tiny circular coloured tablet-style sweets) and Sherbet in a bag.

"Opposite was Bidder Street with Maurice Levine's grocery shop on the corner. He sold a flat slab cake which we called a 'Train Wrecker' and my mam would always say 'Put the cost in the book, I'll pay next week'. Soho Street had a pie shop that filled the air with the smell of the 'Penny Pie Dinners'. Yes, a penny for a pie dinner! I also remember a French Polishing business and Louis Caplin's Sweet Shop. Louis became Lord Mayor of Liverpool.

"Langsdale Street was full of famous boxers who fought at the legendary Liverpool Stadium. Alf Howard, the great knock-out specialist, lived next door to us. I went to St. Francis Xavier's Junior School opposite the Collegiate College and we had a playground on the roof. My dad boxed for the SFX Club in Salisbury Street, where the lads trained in the cellar under the priest's house, at the side of SFX Church. We had photographs of dad in the ring on the wall at home – not by the crack!

"Mum and dad split up and the photos were thrown out and so my own kids and grandchildren don't know what he looked like.

"Your wonderful book helped to spark all of these thoughts. I hope you do another one."

Thank you, James, for your own tremendous memories which are quite humbling in a society in which the size of your new leather sofa can determine your standing in a street, rather than the size of the crack in your wall!

What is it about life in the old inner city districts that gets us all emotional about things like rats, cockroaches, damp back kitchens, steering carts, proper bin men, and debris areas?

St. George's Church pops its head above this Everton street in the Mere Lane area

Clearly, it had nothing to do with the conditions, but everything to do with the community.

I attended a school reunion at the former Major Lester building in Everton Valley and met former class mate Tom Marshall. We were soon revelling in our memories and Tom was in full flow about his personal thoughts. He said:

"We had an infestation of mice in Everton Valley and nearby Mark Street. I can still see my Nan chasing down the entry with a shovel in her hand knocking seven bells out of the little devils to the amusement of the bin men who had disturbed them pulling the bins out of the wall.

"As a youngster, probably about six, I would go up the back entry to the top of Mark Street where the Co-op had their Works Depot. It included a Smithy where all the horses were shod. I would spend hours watching Tom and Sid shoeing the Shires and other giant horses.

"On occasions, I would be invited to sit astride these gentle monsters and ride them down Mark Street, feeling each step on the cobbles as their feet slid. I never thought that I would later be working in the same place as an apprentice."

Like most of us, Tom had a large paper round. He said:

"There was a shop at the bottom of Netherfield Road, near to the Valley. We had to pick the Echos up and carry them to the shop before we started our rounds. It was 77 papers on the late

round as well as 'earlies'. We walked from Mark Street to Patmos Street, for the princely wage of 17 shillings and 6 pence."

My God, Tom, I used to get 2 shillings and sixpence (half a crown) for undertaking the steepest paper round in Everton. You must have been a good negotiator! Tom added: *"You would do your own cash collections as well. Once, my Christmas tips exceeded £10, a princely sum, as wages then were below that for most adults. The shop keeper's daughter was courting the assistant manager of the former Liverpool Stadium. Each Thursday I was given as a bonus six tickets to see the wrestling, Count Bartelli, Billy Two Rivers, Les Kellet, The Royals and so many more. I was the longest serving paper boy at the time."*

I'm surprised Tom is still not doing that round, with its added side benefits, although the famous Liverpool Stadium has long since disappeared. My father used to take me there every Friday night for the big wrestling shows.

Of course, the most famous of the bad boys who prowled around that ring was 'Dirty' Jack Pye.

It seemed as if Jack had been around forever. He was such a famous character that he even had walk-on parts in a series of black and white films including *'Wives Never Know'* in 1936 starring Charlie Ruggles and Mary Boland; *'Leave It to Me'* in 1937 starring Sandy 'Can You Hear Me Mother' Powell; and *'It's a Grand Life'* in 1953 (as a wrestler) starring Frank Randle and Diana Dors.

But Jack was never the support act in the ring, being the star turn everywhere he appeared, not least at the Stadium and Manchester's famous Belle Vue. He was actually born in Bolton in 1903 and so must have been in his fifties when I was booing him at the Stadium. He was actually touching 60 when he quit in 1963, fittingly in Liverpool where he had been such an iconic figure.

A disappointed crowd was given the shock news of Jack's decision to call it a day after they had waited for him to appear at Liverpool Stadium where he was scheduled to fight Billy Two Rivers. In the pre-fight examination the doctor ruled that Jack was in no condition to take to the ring.

Putting your opponents to one side, the Stadium was a dangerous place to be if you were one of the bad boys of wrestling. Little old ladies would use their brollies to jab the anti-heroes as they made their entrance through a baying mob. If Jack was number one, another figure inspired a more obvious hatred in those days.

Hans Streiger was billed as the German 'Blond Bomber' or 'Teutonic Terror' - not the most endearing of nicknames to use in Liverpool after the Second World War. Maybe my memory is playing tricks on me, but I'm sure Hans penned swastikas on his boots and was not averse to giving the Heil Hitler salute to really get the crowd baying for his blood.

In reality, Hans Streiger was Clarke Mellor (and in the early days he did use that name). He was as German as anyone else who comes from New Mills, Derbyshire, but that's wrestling for you.

Those Stadium nights were sensational for young boys, seasoned regulars and little old ladies. We all loved the excitement, the hype and the opportunity to scream blue murder when the likes of Jack Pye started to put the boot in. Then we would all go home and have Horlicks for supper!

Legendary wrestler Jack Pye

The famous Victoria Settlement community centre on Netherfield Road North with the incredibly steep York Terrace rising up behind these workers. This was previously the home of Canon Thomas Major Lester, education pioneer and champion of the poor in Everton

COALMEN, BIN MEN, RAG MEN AND THE REST – STREET THEATRE AT ITS VERY BEST

When the rag man came up the street with his horse and cart, shouting out his presence or alerting you with a bugle, it was as if Christmas had come early

THE age of open fires in houses across Liverpool, and the crucial role of the city's coalmen, has long since passed.

But Mr. A Bolger from Winsford reminded me of the weekly delivery ritual at households all over the city. Mr. Bolger lived in Adelaide Street and Calder Street off Everton's St. Domingo Road. He asked:

"Can anyone remember Ike Askins, the coalman and boxer who always used to take on fighters and win at the Stanley Park Fair which took place once a year?

"He was an old friend of my dad Billy Bolger. Ike had a coal cart with a big horse that tackled those steep Everton streets."

I can't remember Ike, but I have powerful memories of the Hesketh family who had the coal business that served many of those steep Everton streets. I remember Ralph and Jack Hesketh and I'm pretty certain that their coal yard was at the bottom of Beacon Lane.

Of course, all of the houses had open fires and the coal merchants were clearly a key service industry across the city.

I was fortunate enough to be asked to

write the autobiography of former Liverpool Football Club legend Tommy Smith.

Naturally, it was called 'Over The Top – My Anfield Secrets.' Smithy is a great friend of mine, but I never knew that he was actually brought up as a young boy in Everton! Whisper it quietly, the Anfield Iron with strong Everton roots. His early days were actually spent in Buckingham Street which was part of my old Echo paper round. He said that his family lived in rooms above a coalyard.

Tommy was quick to remind me that he had been born in a house in Arkles Lane, Anfield, and that he got an early 'transfer' out of Everton to Lambeth Road, but I never let him forget his roots.

I always felt that they should introduce a new sport into the Olympic Games. I would replace throwing the javelin or putting the shot with throwing a sack of nutty slack down a coal hole! It was certainly more strenuous than the shot put and definitely more skilful than the javelin. Those old coalmen seemed to be able to launch their black gold through a 12 inch circular hole into a black cellar without touching the sides.

We didn't have a cellar and so the lads had to carry their heavy load across the debris at the bottom of Melbourne Street and up a steep back entry, negotiating the narrow back door into the yard while steering clear of the dogs who saw the 'jiggers' as a private access route to their backyard kennels. Dogs and black-faced coalmen never seemed to be the best of friends.

Reflecting on these days, why do I have this inbuilt logic that the summers of my youth were always incredibly hot while every winter was icy cold, delivering snow up to our knees?

June Woodall from Southport recalled:
"The winter of 1947 was one of the severest, not so much for the cold, but because of the fuel crisis.

"People couldn't get coal for their open fires. There was a coal yard in Spellow Lane and the kids would go there and pick up scraps that had fallen from the horse and cart.

Above, a typical rag and bone man.
Below, an old Scott's bakery van

"Certain people were allowed priority coal. These were the lucky ones."

But the coalmen were only one group in a long list when it came to the people who brought goods and services to your front door.

Edward Speakman contacted me to say: *"Don't forget the bloke on the bike who came round every two weeks to sharpen your knives."*

It got me thinking about all of the people who came to our front doors in those days.

My favourite had to be the rag and bone man, whose penetrating cry of "toys for rags" had every kid in the street foaming at the mouth at the thought of getting something new to play with.

It didn't take much to raise our expectations when the prime playthings for a boy at that time might be a bag of ollies, a bow and arrow, five jacks (a game of speed, dexterity and eye co-ordination that could equally be played with five small stones), a battered football, or a diver that sunk to the bottom of a bowl full of water, propelled by some astutely placed bicarbonate of soda. Now all or any of the above could keep any lad occupied throughout the summer. However, there is a limit to the number of times you could watch your tiny diver, bought for sixpence at Woolies, go through his sinking routine.

And so when the rag man, with his horse and cart, came up the street, shouting out his presence or even alerting you with a small bugle, it was as if Christmas had come early.

I recalled in my first 'Lost Tribe' book how my dad, then a small boy in the 1930s, readily swopped his dad's only overcoat for a balloon on a stick! He got more than a tongue lashing before my grandmother set off on a frantic search around the steep streets of Everton to retrieve it.

My favourite toy from the Ragman was a monkey that ran up and down a plastic ladder. It was probably worth just a couple of pence, but it was sheer joy to have something different to play with for half an hour or so.

There was another man who came round in an old van, selling bleach from a cask or tub. The women would keep their old glass bottles and get them filled up. My mother used a Corona lemonade bottle for this purpose once, and stored the bleach in the kitchen sideboard.

I came in from a game of street football desperate for a drink and, yes, you've guessed it. I took a mouthful, but spat it out before I swallowed it. I must have drunk a gallon of water in the next few minutes. You really do wonder how we survived those famous days of our youth.

Of course, horses were still part and parcel of daily life. June Woodall remembers a horse slipping on the ice in Stanley Road, and the carter trying to pull him up again. She said: *"Two or three men, waiting by the tram stop, came across to give him a hand. They even wrapped canvas around the horse's hooves to stop him slipping.*

"We would hang onto the backs of the carts until we reached the stables at the bottom of Athol Street off Commercial Road, and the carter would even let us play in the barn."

I wrote in the Echo about a runaway horse and cart on Scotland Road and sparked an immediate response from Mrs. L. Griffin.

She remembers the winters when the bin men used horses and wagons to collect the refuse, saying: *"I was still at school and our house was in Luther Street off Netherfield Road. We had no back entries on one side. Our backyards were on Ellison Street.*

"One winter, the snow and ice was really bad and the bin wagon was trying to come down Ellison Street. The poor horse slipped and the men had terrible trouble trying to get it back on its feet.

"To make things worse, it happened near the top which was really steep. The bin men really earned their money in those days because they had to get the metal bins from the backyards and carry them down the narrow entries. The bins were heavy, full of ashes from the old coal fires."

Mrs. Griffin also recalled the men who emptied the gas and electric meters, saying: *"They would count all the coins and roll a certain amount in thick paper. My mother would then get some back (which was part of the arrangement). There were four girls in our house and we would watch the man doing his job. We always talk about how heavy the meter man's leather bag must have been as he carried it from house to house.*

"It's a good job it doesn't happen these days because these men would almost certainly be a target.

"We have lovely childhood memories and I despair when I see what is going on these days with the riots and everything. We will never get those days back when the community was all about good neighbours."

Looking down the hill at St. Polycarp's Church on Netherfield Road North with the wall of the John Bagot Hospital on the right, facing Mitford Street. Below the main road are famous streets like Conway and Robsart

EVEN DAREDEVIL EVEL KNIEVEL WOULD THINK TWICE ABOUT RIDING A BIKE DOWN HAVELOCK STREET

"I was born on that hill and we believed the whole world was built on a slant."

IN THE previous chapter I mentioned Tommy Smith's days in Buckingham Street. Jimmy Wheeler was another resident of that street and he wrote to me after reading my description of climbing to the summit of 'Mount Everton' via the notoriously steep Havelock Street. Jimmy said:

"I was born on that hill like you and we believed the whole world was built on a slant (well ours was anyway). We ran up and down that hill four times a day without breaking sweat.

"The only time we strained was when we had to 'push' me Grandma up. Four hands, two on each buttock, as she hauled herself up to Ewbank Street. This was the next street along from Havelock and ran halfway down, stopping at the rear wall of the John Bagot Hospital grounds.

"Vehicles could make the assent by climbing halfway up Havelock then making a right turn before the bollards into the 'opening' before a sharp left up Ewbank to finally make the level sanctuary of Northumberland Terrace. The hospital wall bore witness to the odd burnt out clutch or faulty handbrake.

"My grandparents lived at number one Ewbank which was probably built on Mr James Atherton's former back garden."

Atherton, of course, was the property developer who, in 1814, built a series of streets and mansions on the top of Everton's famous ridge, as well as being the driving force behind St. George's Church.

Jimmy added that when he was at St. George's school, the old caretaker, who lived in a house in the grounds, was known to everyone as POP ATHERTON. He said: *"I wonder if there is a connection?"*

Another member of the 'Lost Tribe' with Havelock Street memories is Jim Fearns.

He wrote to me to say: *"Reading about Havelock Street gave me chills down my spine. I had a friend who lived in this street. My Auntie Bridie lived in the nearby Sir Thomas White Gardens, behind the church of Our Lady Immaculate.*

"A few of the lads made a bet that no one could ride a bike from the top of Havelock to the bottom. I did and my break blocks went on fire. There was smoke everywhere. We had to do it in the night to make sure there were no cars coming when I got to Netherfield Road at the bottom. I was 12/13 at the time.

"The bet was for three 'bob'. Another bet was to walk up, yes walk up, the handrail that ran from bottom to top. And you could only fall off it three times!"

Listen, Jim. I doubt if even the famous American daredevil Evel Knievel, who used to jump 14 buses on his motor bike, would fancy riding down Havelock Street, so I'm impressed to say the least.

A new line in sweets goes on sale in 1959, clearly capturing the attention of these local kids

CHAPTER 21

SWEET MEMORIES ON A TRIP TO THE CORNER SHOP

Sherbert Dabs with their liquorice prodder . . . flying saucers that made your eyes spin

JOHN MORRISON, from the Collegiate-end of Netherfield Road, got me going when he sent me a simple question:

What were the things that sent you into seventh heaven as a kid, walking to school through the old terraced streets of Everton and Scottie, with their little sweet shops on every corner?

John started getting all emotional about the thought of buying four Walkers (toffees) for a penny, or a Penny Arrow Bar.

Then he stepped into the land that time forgot, talking about chewing on a piece of sticky lice (liquorice root) that seemed to last forever. This was the equivalent of chewing on an old twig!

I was immediately transported back in my inner city Time Machine to the days when saying 'Lovely Jubbly' had absolutely nothing to do with David Jason and 'Only Fools and Horses'! And how about those tempting 'Lucky Bags' which promised much and delivered, well, not a lot?

The contents always included several sweets you couldn't stand, and a challenge to put together a five-piece plastic car the size of your little finger, the equivalent of a five-piece jigsaw puzzle. The kids today would be asking where the remote control was.

My grandfather, Adam Wareing, who lived at the opposite end of Netherfield Road to John, introduced me in the early 1950s to my all-time favourite: Fry's Chocolate Cream. Thanks granddad! My mother always had a stash of Walnut Whips in her pantry cupboard. Now let's get the ritual out of the way. Eat the walnut first, bite the pointy end off the swirl of chocolate. Lick out the cream, and then eat the remainder of the chocolate!

John reminded me of those hard Victory V Gums, loose in red tins, unlike the lozenges in the bag. And chewy black jacks that made your tongue look like the far side of the moon.

These boys look set to give us a song on a sweet shop bench while the 'ladies' pose quietly for the camera

absolutely foul and a bitter disappointment to all those of us who loved the 'food drink of the night'.

Far better to *"take a biscuit no bigger than a button. Take a raisin that's been lazin' in the sun. Find yourself a mellow piece of chocolate. Take a TIFFIN - and they're all in one!"*

I must have been a dream target for those marketeers who thought up these slogans.

My mother's friend, Agnes Roberts, had a little sweet shop on Breck Road, gone now, of course. It was famous because it had an old Tin Hat from the war nailed on the wall. Anyone remember it? Jeff Keating from Walton wrote to me about his days in Abbot Street in Everton. He said:

"All the kids used to get pennies and go over to Hamilton Road. A lady would sell toffee apples from her parlour window. As a result, I've only got a couple of my original teeth left! They were brilliant times."

Of course, the old inner streets had shops on every corner from where you could buy just about anything.

Peter Rigby reminded me: *"We moved to Netherfield Road on the corner of Mark Street in 1956. My Nan lived right opposite at number 313. We spent many of our days racing our steeries down 'Neddy Road' or sledging off the hill underneath Devonshire Place.*

"I remember Pop's fish and chip shop; Mrs. Lyons shop where you could get anything from a tin of shoe polish to a gob stopper; the dolls' hospital on Kirkdale Road; going to buy pea shooters and 'catties' (catapults); Nora's sweet shop, later taken over by the Cavanaghs; going to Stanley Park with a bottle of sherbet water and a packet of jam butties; 'Wessie Road' baths for a slipper bath; taking the washing on my steerie to the wash house. So many memories and thank you for helping me revive them."

It's a pleasure Peter. I can smell those fish and chips now, wrapped and eaten in the Echo, of course.

Sherbet Dabs with their liquorice prodder to get to the very bottom of the long pack. Flying saucers that made your eyes spin when you bit through the cardboard outer shell to get to the sugary sherbet inside. Cherry lips that did exactly what it said on the bag. I kept away from those. Cherry lips around our way would get you a good hiding, unless you were a girl, of course!

Then we had Horlicks tablets, which were

Legendary Liverpool manager Bill Shankly went
down to the old Eldon Grove tenements to
cast an eye over this local 'cup final'. Shanks had
a grandstand view on one of the landings and
joined them for a cup of tea after the game

WHAT'S LATIN OR GREEK FOR 'LET'S GO AND HAVE A SLY SMOKE BEHIND THE BIKE SHEDS'?

> We would buy a 'loosie' – usually a 'Woodie' – from John's and smoke it in the shop …

SCHOOL days always inspire incredible memories of the things we used to get up to. Jim Finn lived in the Shaw Street area and in the 1950s attended Liverpool Collegiate where he studied Latin and Greek. Jim recalls: *"It was definitely all Greek to me, and at Collegiate they also played that game with the funny ball.*

"Every Monday, most of the pupils would be given five shillings by their mothers to buy five school dinner tickets, one for each day of the week.

"Quite a few of us would not buy the tickets, opting instead for a large cob for three pence, plus four pennyworth of chips from John's 'chippie' behind the Collegiate. We would rip open the cob and stuff all the chips inside to make a very filling meal.

"With the money left over we would buy a 'loosie' (a single cigarette), usually a Woodbine (aka a 'Woodie') from John's and smoke it in the

shop. One day the shop got raided by the school prefects and those who were not quick enough to get rid of their cigarettes had their names taken. Everybody was ordered out of the shop.

"At Assembly the next morning, the school head, Mr K.A. Crofts, ruled John's chippie out of bounds. John's profits plummeted so much that he made representations to the headmaster and eventually the restriction was removed, with suitable provisos, of course."

Everyone has a different take on school dinners. I very rarely, if ever, had school dinners when I attended Major Lester School on Everton Valley in the mid 1950s. I was happier sprinting home for sandwiches, soup or a boiled egg. The school dinners, as I remember, were not made on the premises, but cooked elsewhere and delivered in big metal containers.

You could smell the cabbage and the carrots a mile off and the potatoes were always tasteless. Just mention the word 'semolina' to me and I get a shiver down my spine. Yet the vast majority of kids were brought up on school dinners.

I have been involved in a few school reunions at Major Lester, and one of the first places we head for is the old canteen hall in the basement. Clearly, even though I wasn't a school dinner connoisseur, I still have this strange affinity with them. It's strange, but even after 50 years I can still smell the cabbage down there. It must be ingrained in the walls, or is it something else?

Kenny Taylor, who has worked at the school for years and is a former pupil, revealed that under the floorboards of the canteen is actually a swimming pool that we never knew about, clearly a key facility ahead of its time when the original Victorian building went up. Obviously, it was never used after the Second World War.

I've now got this bizarre image in my mind of the hidden pool beneath our feet, full of steaming water bringing a thousand cabbages to the boil. So this is how they did it!

Another surprise at our last school reunion was sight of the original school kitchen deep in the building with its old black range still in perfect condition. It came to light when some building work was being done and a wall panel was removed. Wow! That's even better than finding the tomb of Tutankhamun.

Major Lester is awaiting demolition in 2012, a decision that is devastating for its thousands of former pupils. The school name was changed some years ago to Hope Valley and more recently adopted the name 'Four Oaks' which it has taken to new premises on Venmore Street, near to the site of the former Venice Street School in Anfield. Thankfully, the old kitchen range has gone as well, not to cook the modern school dinners on, but as a perfect visual memory of the old Major Lester.

If they did choose to bring the range back to life, I might even give the cabbage a try, but definitely not the semolina!

As I organised the last reunion, I received a tremendous letter from Mrs. Edna Pugh (nee Skelly) who left the old Everton Valley school in 1935 at the age of 15.

Edna wrote:

"I am now 90 years of age and I have wonderful memories of Major Lester. I remember the bungalow where we had cookery, and the Domestic Science classes underneath the school.

"I remember coming out of school and running down Sherlock Street into the arms of the lovely policeman who saw us across Walton Breck Road. I was born and brought up in Gorst Street off Blessington Road, and what a lovely childhood I had."

That's the one thing we always used to envy the girls for, Edna. They would come out after cookery, with a neat cloth covering their wicker baskets, hiding something with a heavenly smell, some scones or an apple pie.

At secondary school, I was never any good at the boys' options like woodwork and metalwork. I made a wooden toast rack once and a three-legged coffee table that was never finished. Half a dozen current scones

John's Chippie on Conway Street

would have been a much more sensible option. As one of those kids who occasionally suffered the cringe factor wearing home knitted jumpers in the 1950s which never quite matched the official school colours, or always took on a baggy feel, especially when it rained, I just loved the memory submitted by Kath Binnion of Winsford. She told me: *"I was born in Windsor Road, Tuebrook, but unfortunately my mum died when I was seven. Dad was serving in the War in Burma at the time, so my three sisters and I were put away in homes for six years. I was the youngest at seven, but I was away from my elder sisters.*

"Doreen was the next to youngest, and we were evacuated to Elscot Homes in Mossley Hill. Thankfully, we were later all together again with our grandmother, old Granny Scott, who was well known in Tuebrook. We lived in Marlborough Road and I attended Lister Drive School.

"I remember the day when the whole school was assembled for a photo in the hall. This gave me a problem. I needed a new gymslip because my old one was too short, so I cut out the shoulders and sewed new pieces in. The problem was they were two different colours.*

"I then knitted myself a jumper to cover up. The photo required all the girls down one side of the staircase, and all the boys down the other. I was shouted at from both sides to take my jumper off as all the girls had white blouses on.

"I just couldn't do it because of the shame. When the photo eventually arrived, there was me, sitting in my home-knitted maroon jumper for all to see. As a 13-year-old, the embarrassment stayed with me for years."

Kath should not worry. We have all been there. We relied on our mothers to be world-champion knitters, and she should be proud to have had the instinct to get out the needles herself! That deserved an A-level certificate in its own right!

Is there anybody there? These boys are fishing for tiddlers and tadpoles in a park lake.
The patch in the pants (second right) indicate this was still the era of 'make and mend'

CHAPTER 23

ROOFTOP DOGS, MONKEYS UP CURTAINS – AND JAM JARS FULL OF FROGS AND TADPOLES

We had this knack of adding to the number of pets in our small terraced houses – jam jars came back with all manner of mini creatures

TOM KIRBY is a former Major Lester boy who lived on Everton Valley. I've never known anyone with such pin-sharp recollections of his childhood than Tom and many of his stories will help bring alive our childhood memories on subsequent pages.

Tom was telling me about the days when the Orange Lodges would gather at the bottom of Netherfield Road near the Midland Bank, and some played whilst waiting for the procession to set off. Tom recalled:

"The houses there were tiny and at the back the 'oller' was raised about four feet near the backyard walls which were only about six feet high and a flagstone's width away.

"My dog Sniffy, a black and white Border Collie, used to jump the gap and then get onto the low roofs before making his way to the top apex. Like a wolf, he would howl for ages as the bands played. He always chose Mrs. Evans house (mother of my friend Dave Evans) and she would come out and shout 'Anybody seen Tommy Kirby to get his dog off my roof?'

"I would be hidden, pressed hard against a wall shaking my head vigorously to everyone to say: 'No Mrs. Evans'.

"The dog would still be up there howling away when the bands had long left and gone on their march. Dave and the Evans family moved away in the 'clearances' and we lost touch completely.

"Forty years later I met up with Dave again at a Major Lester School reunion in 2003 and we renewed our friendship.

"Unfortunately, just two years later, Dave passed away. I went to his service in a little village in Yorkshire and saw Mrs. Evans from a distance in the front pews of the church. I sat way back and she didn't see me, even though she would not have recognised me after 45 years.

"We were all invited to the local Hall for the 'wake' and I went to pay my respects. I met an ex-classroom mate from my primary school days and was chatting away in a group in the middle of the Hall when I saw the front door opening for family members, including Mrs. Evans .

"Suddenly a voice spoke out: 'Tommy Kirby — you and your bloody dog!' Mrs. Evans had recognised me after all that time and on a day of such dire circumstances had remembered Sniffy. Mrs. Evans was always a lovely lady (except when angered by a howling dog on her roof). Ha ha!"

That is a great memory, Tom. I can well remember a more general cry of exasperation from inner city parents: 'Kids, cats and bloody dogs!' That put us all in the same frame of being delightful one minute and absolutely uncontrollable the next.

We also had this knack of adding to the number of pets in our small terraced houses, usually after a day out at Freshfield, Ainsdale or Formby. Jam jars came back with all manner of mini creatures.

Many mothers, about to clean the front steps, would have wondered where their bucket had gone, only to find it in the backyard full of tadpole spawn, never a pretty sight.

Days later it would be full of tadpoles darting from one side to the other and the bucket would have to remain commandeered by an eager ten-year-old boy who would

I couldn't give a monkey's! This dog looks relaxed around his unexpected new friend

then create an island of half bricks from the local debris to complete the final phase of the exercise, a platform for the frogs and newts to climb on.

What did these amphibians think when they suddenly realised they were being brought up in a mop bucket, and in a slum clearance area as well! We can only speculate. Like everyone else, they were probably hoping for the offer of a new home in the suburbs.

Did someone say *Norris Green?* That sounds like somewhere that must have a lake or a pond. Put me down for a transfer to Walton Hall Park.

My pal Graham Jennings, who lived on the corner of Netherfield Road and Melbourne Street, always went one better.

His dad Eddie was brilliant at building things, making us a high jump for our very own debris Olympics, a table tennis table for the cellar, and a large wooden container in the backyard for Graham's tropical tree frogs.

When the 'clearances' started, those frogs were probably demanding a transfer to one of the posh housing estates in somewhere like Allerton!

Of course, even more exotic animals found their way into our terraced houses, not least straight after the Second World War when many sailors brought monkeys back from god knows where. Now I've got a couple of questions here:

Fancy a drink? I'll have mine 'on the rocks'. Lost Tribe author Ken Rogers (left) and friend
Mal Smith on an away day from the terraced streets of Everton in the 1960s

1. Where do you draw the line here as a commanding officer? Would it have been okay for a homeward bound soldier or sailor to walk an elephant up the gang plank of the Empress of Scotland in Calcutta Docks with a tag round its neck saying *Pier Head, Liverpool?*

Or how about a hissing cobra in a wicker basket, ready to rear its head and perform a hypnotic dance to a mouth organ rendition of 'Maggie May'?

Imagine bringing it home to a tiny terraced house off Roscommon Street and forgetting to put the lid on the basket after a night down at the pub. You go to spend a penny in the outside toilet, strolling down the backyard with your candle and a copy of the Echo.

Is this all getting too much for you?

2. And what about those monkeys? What was the train of thought that led someone to think: "Perfect pet for a terraced house on the steep streets of Everton with all those lampposts to climb! Me ma' won't mind if it thinks the parlour curtains are the equivalent of a jungle vine. And it can sleep in the kennel in the backyard with Dinky the dog. No problem."

I've seen a monkey up the curtains in the parlour and, believe me, it wasn't singing the theme song from Jungle Book. The cat wasn't too happy either.

So Tommy Kirkby's dog Sniffy, howling to the moon on a backyard wall, all seems quite benign in the circumstances. But tell that to Mrs. Evans.

REPAIRING OLD 'CASIES' AND USING A RED HOT POKER ON THOSE FAMOUS PLASTIC FRIDO BALLS

We went through plastic ball after ball, but we had just one leather 'casey' which was saved for special matches against other street teams

GIRLS play football in their thousands these days, but back in the 1950s 'footy' was strictly for the boys.

Well, I say that. I met an old neighbour, Tom Johnson, at one of my street reunion events at St. George's Church, and he revealed that my mother could dribble and shoot with the best of them as a kid when the ball came out in her street.

Why doesn't that surprise me?

May (Wareing) Rogers was equally adept at putting up shelves, solving minor electrical problems, mending shoes, painting and decorating and handling anything else that might be thrown at her.

She was also the best curtain maker in Liverpool after working for years in Frost's Store on Walton Road (but that's going off the subject). It's enough to say that I should not have been surprised that she put some of the lads to shame when it came to 'footy'.

Maybe I got my passion for the great game from her, although in my first 'Lost Tribe' book I highlighted how my father Harry joined the boys in the street for an impromptu game one day and hammered a superb volley right through the window of next door neighbour Edna Sawyers.

She was fuming and so was my mother who immediately demonstrated to Dad how you should get your instep over the ball to keep it low when you are driving a shot towards goal!

Of course, the key to any game was having a ball in the first place. Tommy Kirby, he of the howling dog, recalls: "We used to club together to buy the plastic footballs at 1/11 1d each. The kids would put in a penny or up to threepence to play the street football matches. The trouble was, there was the traffic up and down Netherfield Road and the balls would burst under the cars.

"There was also the barbed wire surrounding the woodyard in Mark Street, plus thousands of small pieces of glass, or sharp stones to do the same. We went through plastic ball after ball, but we had just one leather 'casey' which was saved for special matches against other street teams (not internal street games). We would also use this ball on the marked out and goal posted GRASS pitches at Clubmoor Rec where once in a while an extra special 'rivals' street match would be played – a bus trip away.

"That 'casey' could also get burst, but just round the corner and opposite the Dolls' Hospital on Kirkdale Road was a man who stiched the leather panels back together for us for just sixpence a time.

"I often wonder now in adulthood whether he charged such a small sum for the work because he knew of our plight and our love for our most 'treasured' possession – and the joy that lovely leather panelled ball brought to all our lives.

"All we had to do then was put a bicycle patch over the inner rubber bladder and inflate it. The 'casey' would then be put away in the cupboard, ready for our next 'special' match.

"That cross lace was prominent and took your forehead off if you headed it. The leather ball was also like a rock to the head when wet, but nobody pulled out of the headers. Those balls were character building. Could you stay on your feet in front of your pals and the opposition while feeling so dizzy and nauseous after the ball had come down from 50 feet up in the air for a header? Great, great days."

My own memories of those treasured caseballs takes me back to my former high school, Evered Avenue, where I became school sports captain. It was my job every Friday to 'dubbin' six balls ready for the school matches the following day. Dubbin was a wax product used to soften and waterproof leather and other materials. It was a mixture of natural wax, oil and tallow and had a unique, pungent smell.

I would dip my hands into this huge tin of reddy brown dubbin and rub it into the leather panels of the footballs. They would be

A pre-match warm-up on Conway Street

given more tender love and care than a full body massage in a Turkish bath, not that I've had any experience of the latter, of course!

Each captain would come to the sports room to take responsibility for his team's caseball until its prompt return the following Monday. I would count them out and count them in again for our brilliant sports master Ken Webster – and a lost ball was worse than a lost match.

I would wash my hands a hundred times after every 'casey' session, but they would still smell of dubbin days later. All over the city, boys would also be dubbining their leather football boots. What a dream moment it was for lads from the concrete jungle to be able to play on grass with a proper leather football. Tom is right. We treated those 'special' caseballs with the reverence they deserved.

But most of the time we played in the street with a 'plassy' equivalent. These were often cheap with thin skins which made them too light for real football. A solid shot would 'balloon' high over the bar, caught by the lightest gust of wind. These balls were totally vulnerable to any small shard of glass on a debris or oller. Suddenly they would be as flat as a pancake and totally useless for the 'cup finals' we played on a daily basis, sometimes two a side but often full scale battles involving players of all different abilities and ages.

My pal Graham Jennings would always be a famous goalkeeper, Ron Springett of Sheffield Wednesday and England; Alan Hodgkinson of Sheffield United and England; – Peter Bonetti ('The Cat') of Chelsea, another full international; or Manchester City's German goalkeeping legend Bert Trautmann who once courageously played on in an FA Cup Final after breaking his neck.

We would be reliving these historic moments within minutes of the final whistle.

Funnily enough, I can never remember us wanting to be one of the Everton or Liverpool goalkeepers, but the Fifties were pretty barren for both of our big clubs. These were the days when it was possible to be an avid Merseyside Red or Blue, and still have a great admiration for one of the top stars of a leading rival.

Of course, there was no football on television at that time, other than the Cup Final once a year. This was the day when we would emerge from an afternoon in front of Graham's 14-inch black and white telly to take on the mantle of the hero of the hour.

And so I would want to be Stan Matthews, hero of 1953; Peter McParland of Aston Villa (1957) and Nat Lofthouse of Bolton Wanderers (1958) who shoulder charged Manchester United's Ray Wood into the back of the net as the goalkeeper caught the ball under the posts, one of Wembley's most controversial moments.

Of course, on other non Cup Final days I would have to be the swashbuckling Dave Hickson of Everton, Fred Pickering, Bobby Collins, Billy Bingham or Tommy Ring. You will recognise that they all wore royal blue. I would be thrilled and honoured to actually partner Dave Hickson up front when his

St. George's School playground in the Fifties on a day when all the girls brought in their treasured prams

Goodison days were long gone and we both played under the managership of Ivor Scholes for the famous charity team – the 'Over The Hill Mob'. I can assure you that the Cannonball Kid was never over the hill, even when he pulled on a shirt in his sixties!

But I digress from being the 'voice of the balls' to steal the Lottery man's mantle. Those thin plastic footballs I was talking about would ultimately be replaced by the classic 'Frido' that could also be re-inflated using a simple bicycle pump when it had been kicked and headed so many times, that the air inside began to give up the ghost. I have to say that even the 'Frido' was not totally immune to a debris puncture, but there was always an instant solution.

We would race into the house where the open fire was always burning brightly in the grate. The poker would be thrust into the flames until it was red hot. It was then a simple case of smoothing over the plastic where the puncture had occurred, whipping out the bike pump and bringing the ball back to the right pressure. Within minutes we were back in business.

Of course, all street footballers will remember that this emergency repair often led to a large egg appearing on the side of the ball which had the effect of making it swerve without any side spin. Who needed to be a Brazilian when you had an old and battered 'Frido' ball?

CHAPTER 25

HOW WOULD
JENSON BUTTON
HAVE COPED IN
THE EVERTON
GRAND PRIX?

Once a 'steerie' set off down one of Everton's steep streets there was simply no turning back

I HAVE tremendous respect for Grand Prix drivers who power round the world's most famous racing circuits. It takes incredible courage to climb inside one of those dream machines and go wheel to wheel with rivals at over 200 miles per hour. Every time I watch Jenson Button battling for victory, he gets my total admiration.

But then I always smile and wonder how Jenson would have coped aboard one of the thousands of wooden steering carts built by young boys in the incredibly steep streets of Everton and other inner city districts. I am always reminded of this when people share their 'steerie' memories on the 'Lost Tribe of Everton' website.

For the uninitiated, the body of a steering cart was effectively a long plank of wood, sitting above a set of old pram wheels. The wheels at the back were often larger than those at the front, but now I'm getting a bit high tech for Jenson Button's support team!

Once a 'steerie' set off down one of Everton's steep streets there was simply no turning back for a fairly simple reason. There was no brake, or at least one that made any difference! The words that appear on the site are fairly universal:

"We would gather speed as we sped downhill – no brakes on our carts – towards the main road. Only a very tight right hand 90 degree turn would avoid us crashing under the wheels of a bus or lorry.

"You had to avoid the unfortunately placed lamp posts and many a cart would be totally wrecked against that hazard for going too wide on the pavement and failing to get back over to the inside. You would then continue headlong downhill towards the tight right hand corner (to avoid the main road junction further down) and into the sandpit to stop your wheels dead and jar you to a sudden full stop.

"We even had 'stewards' to avoid us crashing into ordinary people walking up that side of Netherfield Road. Of course, it was okay for participants to endanger themselves."

There was only one activity that matched our thrilling steering cart escapades. This was the 'Slide of death on a sheet of black ice' which was naturally part of the annual Everton Winter Olympics.

As a former sports editor, I've often heard it pronounced that the world's most dangerous sport is the bobsleigh, a winter test in which teams of two or four make timed runs down a narrow, twisting and steep banked ice descent.

Let me put it this way. Take all of the above, and add in an indiscriminate scattering of snow-covered half bricks while attempting the 'run' down one of the steep streets of Everton – not on a super strong steel sled that has been scientifically tried and tested by a Swiss army captain in a wind tunnel – but rather on a piece of tin found cast aside on a debris, or more likely astride a sheet of wet cardboard that felt as if it might disintegrate beneath you at any given moment.

You had to throw in the potential for your 'timed run' going 'off pist' as we used to say round our way. Your self-made sled might swerve off the debris track onto an ice-bound

street and into the path of any passing car or lorry that might be stupid enough to try and climb Mount Everton in the winter.

I well remember playing in Melbourne Street with my cousin Alan Wareing. He was on our improvised sled during one of those typical winters of the 1950s.

He started to gather pace, which is not very hard when you are on a street-long sheet of black ice – with me running behind, trying to keep up. Suddenly a coal lorry turned up the street off Netherfield Road and I just managed to clip Alan's back and send him spinning to a halt in the gutter.

There you have it . . . THE most dangerous sport in the world – and don't let anyone tell you any different, confirmed by Glynn

These lads must have been from the posh end of the street – we used to slide on pieces of tin or even cardboard

Hewitson. He is one of many who swopped information on the *Lost Tribe of Everton* website, asking if anyone remembered the side of the Mere Lane Cinema which was quite steep.

He said: *"When it snowed we always made a slide from top to bottom which ended up like glass. Kids came from everywhere to have a go on it.*

"We must have filled the accident and emergency department every winter. It's amazing no one was killed, especially when you carried on past the end of the slide into the road.

"In summer we also made those steering carts and used the same side of the cinema. We must have hit 40 miles an hour. It's a wonder anyone made it safely into the cinema."

The 'slide of death on a sheet of black ice' was naturally part of the annual Everton Winter Olympics

36 JACK SHARP 36
Dunlop
Childrens Shoes
A and
FOOTWEAR FOR CHILDREN

QUEUEING AROUND THE BLOCK FOR THOSE PRECIOUS FOOTIE TICKETS AND THE JUNGLE THAT WAS THE BOYS' PEN

> I grew up with those giant stadia as a backdrop to my early life and as a small boy I could hear the roar of the crowd from our house

A huge crowd queues outside Jack Sharp's Whitechapel shop for tickets for the Liverpool v Everton game in September 1946

I'M OFTEN reminded about those legendary days when we queued up for football tickets outside Goodison Park or Anfield.

Whenever there was a big match, lads from all over the city would be put on 'queue duty' to earn a few bob. These snaking lines of football fans seemed to stretch into infinity and there was always a fear that the Box Office window would be slammed shut just when you were finally in sight of that prized and all-important match ticket for a much-anticipated derby game or a massive cup tie.

Let's remember that crowds after the Second World War were massive, to say the least. Over 78,000 people inspired a record attendance at Everton's Goodison Park on 18 September, 1948, just a few months before I was born, although I expect it was all 'pay at the gate' in that era.

For the record, captains Alex Stevenson of Everton and Jackie Balmer of Liverpool led the teams out side by side to play out a 1-1 draw. Take a look at the picture of this remarkable occasion. The two key men are both balding and looking more like a pair of old grandfathers than soccer superstars.

However, let me quickly add that both were great characters and superb players, Stevenson was a diminutive playmaker while Balmer was a free-scoring centre forward who once bagged a hat-trick of hat-tricks in Liverpool's 1946/47 Championship season.

In this soccer mad era, crowds of 50,000 plus were not so much the exception as the rule. Attendances would fall off as the Fifties failed to deliver any tangible glory for our Big Two, but the rivalry of the famous Harry Catterick and Bill Shankly sides of the Sixties ensured that the mega ticket queues were now a regular occurrence, something that was highlighted by Tommy Kirby who lived within shouting distance of both grounds.

A record crowd at Goodison Park on 18 September, 1948

He said: *"In our early teens we gained 'pocket money' by going up to Anfield or Goodison where men would give us a ten shilling note to buy two FA Cup tickets (or replay tickets). They would point at a house or a pub and say 'I'm in there when you get them', or 'drop them in that shop with Eddy' or whatever.*

"We would queue for anything from half an hour to four hours to get to the front and buy our tickets at, say, three bob each (15p each in modern money). The four shillings change was ours to keep for queuing.

"We then went round again if we could for someone else. If we got two lots in a day or night or BOTH teams were selling tickets in a week, we were rich indeed. We never reneged on the deals ever.

"Thinking now, in hindsight, how different were the attitudes then? Everyone trusted everyone else. That money sure helped in the household. I often tried to get a treat for my mum, something she liked but hardly ever saw. A favourite food or item. I also bought some of my clothes with my queueing 'wages' so that helped her family budget too."

As a sports journalist, I've been in the privileged position of having a seat in the press boxes at Goodison and Anfield for most of my working life. However, like Tommy I was born within a stone's throw of both grounds, attending Major Lester School on Everton Valley and playing all of my early school football in Stanley Park.

I grew up with those giant stadia as a permanent backdrop to my early life and as a small boy I could hear the roar of the crowd from our house on a Saturday afternoon when the teams emerged or when a goal went in. It was a comforting sound, like hearing the One O'clock Gun, which reminded us that all was well with the world.

I've been in one of those giant ticket queues that stretched round the ground and out of sight, feeling total elation when finally claiming that prized ticket. Of course, like most kids at that time, and many adults who couldn't afford the admission price, entry into both Goodison and Anfield would often happen at three quarter time when they opened the gates.

It seemed to me as if there were as many people going in at that late point as there were coming out. This is how you earned your spurs as a young fan, standing alongside the adults who would often pass the smaller kids over their heads to the front.

Of course, you started your career as a football fan in one of the Boys' Pens where the high pitched roar indicated that several hundred highly charged juveniles were in full flow, learning the ropes and copying the chants of the adults.

The Pen wasn't a pleasant place to be at times, not so much a playground as a jungle. Lads would try and climb over the high steel fence that separated the lads from the dads, only to be pushed back in by the zealous stewards. Fighting, or rather posturing, was a regular occurrence, but most of the time we were joined by a common loyalty to the Reds or the Blues, in my case the latter – coming from an Everton family that stretched back to the days when Everton played in Stanley Park as St. Domingo's.

I was fortunate enough to be asked to write 'Goodison Glory' – the official history of Everton's famous stadium, and I have written several books on the Reds including the 'Official Liverpool FC Hall of Fame'. Many fans cannot understand how it is possible to cross the divide, but it's the business I am in.

Jamie Carragher and Michael Owen were both Evertonians before starring for the Reds. Peter Reid and Dave Watson were both avid Liverpudlians before winning Championship medals with the Blues.

I have one Evertonian son and one fanatical son who is a Kop season ticket holder, but there is the modern difference.

In my day, you always followed the team your father and grandfather supported, come what may. And mine were royal blue through and through.

Pictured in 1946, the wholesale vegetable
and fruit market inside the North Market
at the end of Great Homer Street

CHAPTER 27

'GREATY' TRAIL FOR SALT FISH BREAKFAST, SUGAR BUTTY LUNCH AND MAGICAL CAKE TEA

We always got the same treat for Sunday tea — a box of cakes, blackcurrant tart, creme bun, trifle, custard slice, custard tart, Eccles cake — seventh heaven!

I'VE NEVER been a great shopper, but then most men would rather have their teeth pulled out than trek from one store to another in search of a bargain. However, up to the age of ten I had no choice but to trail in the wake of my energetic mother as she set off on her regular Saturday shopping safari the length and breadth of Great Homer Street.

This exercise started in the Co-op at the Kirkdale Road end of 'Greaty' and finished in the world famous open air market at the other end. The distance is less than a mile, but it always seemed like a full marathon.

Pat Davies lived in Kirkdale Road. She said: *"Yes, every Saturday was 'Greaty' day. I also went with my mum while my dad looked after the little ones. We did it the other way round, going to the market first, picking through the second hand clothes looking for bargains. There was no help then, not that my mum and dad would have taken it!*

"A pound of mixed biscuits from Woolies, blood oranges, liver, marg, sugar (for the sugar butties) . . . maybe a heart for Sunday dinner, potatoes and veg. One day a week we had blind Scouse (without meat!) This was the menu of our life. Oh, and I almost forgot the salt fish."

JI 6800

Salt fish, Pat, with a nob of 'marge' on the top, of course. We thought we were posh when Stork Margarine came out with its soft, white texture (and its claim to be just like butter). Stork replaced the solid block of yellow Echo margarine we had previously used. We only had 'best butter' on Sundays. What a treat.

But back to 'Greaty' and those never-ending Saturdays.

Mum seemed to know everyone and would always stop for a chat while I just stared into the middle distance, wishing I was back in the street playing football.

Of course, she had my attention when we went into Sayers where we always got the same treat for Sunday tea. *A box of cakes: blackcurrant tart, crème bun, trifle, custard slice, custard tart, Eccles cake.* It doesn't take much to launch you into seventh heaven!

Incidentally, we always asked for an *'ekless'* cake rather than an *'ekels'* cake which would amuse people from the town of Eccles!

Tom Kirby's shopping memories stretch slightly beyond 'Greaty'. He recalls:
"My Mum and me (aged seven onwards) pushed an old pram from the Valley down Boundary Street to some kind of furnace place, and we bought two large sacks of coke which we had to fill ourselves. The coke went on top of the coal on the fire at home to make it last a lot longer - all through the night in fact - and the coal was far more expensive, so the coke 'padded' it out well.

"Then, as we came up Boundary Street to the top end near Scottie Road, I waited outside with the pram while she went in and claimed her big plain white labelled tins, half with orange on them and half with dried egg. These were both in powdered form that you added water to. It was the government's way of giving kids nutrients after the war."

How did we survive, Tom? Probably with another box of Sayers cakes!

When I penned a Liverpool Echo column about the great characters of the street

'Lascars' – Indian seamen

districts, it inspired a follow-up letter from reader June Woodall. She recalled:
"I remember the Indian seamen. They were called Lascars and when their ships docked they would walk up to Scotland Road and Paddy's Market on a shopping spree.

"They seemed very strange at the time. They couldn't speak English and some wore skirts and were barefoot. They also had a funny way of walking, raising each foot high in the air and then bringing them down flat.

"My future husband helped out in a bicycle shop that sold everything from radios to tyres, pumps and old motor bike parts. The Lascars, or 'Johnnies' as we called them, just loved this shop and a lot of wheeling and dealing went on.

"One of them bought a motor bike helmet and the gauntlets to go with it. He put them on and walked all the way back to the ship like that. We were all helpless with laughter and he was laughing too.

"This was just before the war ended and food was scarce. The Lascars would nearly cause a riot on Saturday mornings when they tried to buy full crates of apples (no oranges then). The local

A busy scene at a Liverpool barrow in 1968

women in the queue at the fruit shops would be going berserk and threatening the shopkeeper because everything was still rationed then. They would tell the Lascars how many apples they could have and peace would be restored."

June's memories reminded me of the international sailors buying goods in the markets, not least hats and bicycle parts. You would see them walking back to the docks with several hats on their heads, and half a bike, or a couple of wheels under their arms. No doubt these were highly valued when they got back home.

June also mentioned a few old street phrases in her letter to me, and this had Echo reader James Maher reminding me of one of his mother's favourites when she got mad with her two daughters.

She would say: *"I'll swing for you Cow Ann."*

James recalled the nicknames for some of the characters in his street. *'Al Jolson'* would go to work in the morning clean as a whistle and come home for tea with a face full of soot. Then there was *'File'* who would file half pennies down to fit the gas meter.

Finally, a great old phrase was sent to me from Mr. D. Hogg of Walton who recalled his mother's favourite whenever he borrowed money:

"I suppose I'll get it back when Donnelly docks!"

This refers to the ship the *Richard Donnelly*, which is said to have sunk in Liverpool Bay. A model of the 'Donnelly' is inside St. Nicholas' Church at the Pier Head. The church is linked to another famous Liverpool phrase: *"I'll be waiting till Dick docks",* meaning "I'll be waiting a long time".

NOTICE

A child sits on the pavement of
Mountjoy Street with the view
behind onto Netherfield Road
and Arkwright Street in 1949.
Inset, the One O'Clock Gun at
Morpeth Dock, Birkenhead

CHAPTER 28

NO NEED FOR A WATCH OR CLOCK WHEN WE HAD THE ONE O'CLOCK GUN

Audible right across the city, it alerted kids like me that it was time to end my lunch break and head back to school

THERE are constant headlines in the Liverpool Echo these days about gun incidents around the city and it makes for demoralising reading.

However, gunfire could be heard every day across the inner city communities when I was growing up and while the Police heard it and knew who the 'culprits' were, they never bothered to make a single arrest!

I hand over to Alice Wise, 84, who is living in Woolton these days, but is a fully paid up member of the 'Lost Tribe of Everton & Scottie Road'. She reminded me of that every day occurrence in the Fifties and Sixties, the firing of the legendary One 'O Clock Gun.

Alice explained: *"I spent most of my childhood and teenage years in Clarence Grove off Heyworth Street. The bin-men would come every Tuesday with their horse and cart. My mother always had the shovel and bucket ready for me, and after dinner I had to stay close to the horse, waiting for the One 'O Clock Gun to go off.*

"I don't know if it was the fright, or what, but the horse would always do what it had to do as soon as it heard the sound of the Gun. I would be standing by to collect the manure to spread on the rhubarb.

"My mother said it would give us bright eyes and a clear brain. Of course, we had to believe her."

For anybody born after the 1960s, I should explain that the One O'Clock Gun was a Liverpool institution for close on a century, audible right across the city and alerting kids like me that it was time to end my lunch break and head back to school, while enabling people in offices, factories and dockyards to accurately check their watches and clocks.

A cannon positioned at Morpeth Dock, Birkenhead was fired remotely from Bidston Observatory at one o'clock each working day, triggered electrically by a specially adapted Robert Molyneux clock.

On the dockside, the cannon, a relic from the Crimean wars, was loaded, and at 12.30pm a member of staff tested the connection

between the clock at the Observatory and the cannon. At one second to one o'clock the switch would be thrown at the Observatory, the firing being triggered by the next swing of the clock's pendulum. On clear days the flash could be spotted from across the Mersey.

This service was performed from 1867 until July 18th, 1969, apart from a break during the Second World War.

Alice went on to tell me: *"We also had a dog called Mickey. He had a cough, so my mother pulled one of my brother's jumpers over his front paws, crossed it over his back and fastened it with a pin. Mickey followed me to school. A policeman said: 'Is that your dog?' I was terrified and said: 'No sir, it's my mother's'.*

"He asked why the dog was wearing a jumper and I explained he had a cough. He asked how we were treating it and I explained my mother was giving the dog warm milk and a Beecham's Powder. He said 'Tell your mother never to let this dog out again unless he has got his trousers on!

"I ran all the way home thinking I'd done something wrong, much to the amusement of everyone."

A tantalising peep over an Everton
backyard wall with its familiar outside toilet
and a sink where this lady did her washing

Opposite page: A friendly 'Bobby' helps
these kids to cross a busy Scotland Road

UNCLE CHARLIE'S
LUNATIC ASYLUM

– With apologies to the Co-op laundry!

HERE'S a conundrum that most people of a certain age in Liverpool will instinctively know the answer to: Why did we go to the Lunatic Asylum to get our clothes cleaned?

Doris Mousdale, formerly Doris Rimmer and brought up in Conyers Street in Everton, wrote to me to say how the 'Lost Tribe of Everton & Scottie Road' book had stirred some wonderful memories for her, not least because she lives 'Down Under' these days in Auckland, New Zealand. Doris told me:

"People will still remember the UCLA (Uncle Charlies Lunatic Asylum), otherwise known as the Co-op laundry. They called to collect the tablecloths and sheets, taking them on a Monday bringing them back wrapped in a brown paper parcel on Thursdays. This service was replaced by the launderette in Great Homer Street and then again by twin tub washing machines."

Doris may be as far from Netherfield Road North as you can get these days, but this has only served to hone her remarkable memory.

They will certainly strike a chord with many of you. She told me:

"I can remember the full shopping list for Sykes on the corner of Netherfield Road North and Mitylene Street where we bought our groceries. I also remember Billy Holmes' store on the corner

CHAPTER 29

Some of the famous UCLA laundries including the
Heyworth Street branch (left)

of Crete Street which had huge crates of Fernleaf
butter. Billy would cut half a pound off for you, but
we also had them delivered by Mr. Edwards from
Edwards the Grocers in Great Homer Street.

"It was close by the ice cream parlour where we
used to drive to from Conyers Street to pick up a
bowl (2/6 worth) to go with the strawberries we had
during the summer months.

"This was replaced by the ice cream man who
came each night with his pushbike and dry ice to
keep the lolly ices and ice cream sandwiches cold.

"Then the ice cream vans started coming as
regular as clock work at six o' clock each night. My
father was known to follow a Mr. Whippy van to
get his fix of ice cream and one of the reasons he
took us to the Tatler Cinema in the city centre on
Sundays was for the 6d tubs of ice cream.

"The Liverpool Echo and former Evening Express
were delivered at night by an old guy who picked
them up and delivered them around the houses.
He had an extra run for the Pink Echo on Saturday
nights.

"R. L. Martindale from Crown Street delivered the
coal and we were made to stand at the top of the
cellar stairs when it was being poured down the grid
into the cellar to count the five bags and to check it
was good coal and not all 'slack'.

"Our milk was delivered by Hansens, three pints
a day and five on Sundays with a bottle of cream.
I can remember the excitement when they added

A clean sweep on
Potter Street

orange juice and Wall's Sausages to their milk floats, but I don't think they lasted long.

"The Jaxo man called each week with Jaxo and bleach. My mother got through gallons of the stuff. He also delivered when we moved to West Derby."

Doris also recalled that household jobs for girls included scrubbing the backyard steps before graduating to the front door steps. She said:

"For boys it was chopping wood or whitewashing the backyard walls, and collecting lemonade bottles and jam-jars to get money back at the rag and bone merchants.

"The Docks, Jacobs and Hartleys were amongst the big employers. Some families had five or six people working at Tates Sugar Refinery near the Dock Road, working shifts of 2-10 or 6-2.

"People didn't have a lot. My mother used to send food across to our neighbours – bread puddings, soup or tins of corned beef.

"What you had you shared, including clothes, particularly black coats and hats for funerals. A good respectful send off was all part of the culture.

"I remember concerts at the Victoria Settlement community centre; all day in Stanley Park; penny Vantas drinks; walking to the city centre Museum and Art Gallery on Sundays; being able to recite the order of the Liverpool Docks; toffee apples in September; playing two balls and tops and whips; games like skipping, kick the can, pie-crust coming over, and rounders; cricket, and footie for the boys, all on very steep streets; and mums sitting on the steps 'jangling' after tea, while watching the kids play."

And what wonderful memories they are, Doris.

The original Mr. Whippy

'Make and Mend' was a wartime campaign to help people deal with shortages in every area of daily life

The famous Duffy's store on 'Greaty' at the bottom of Rose Vale where you could buy just about anything. Inset, an old cobbler puts new studs in a football boot

CHAPTER 30

A LOAD OF OLD COBBLERS? NO, OUR SHOE REPAIRERS WERE REAL HEROES

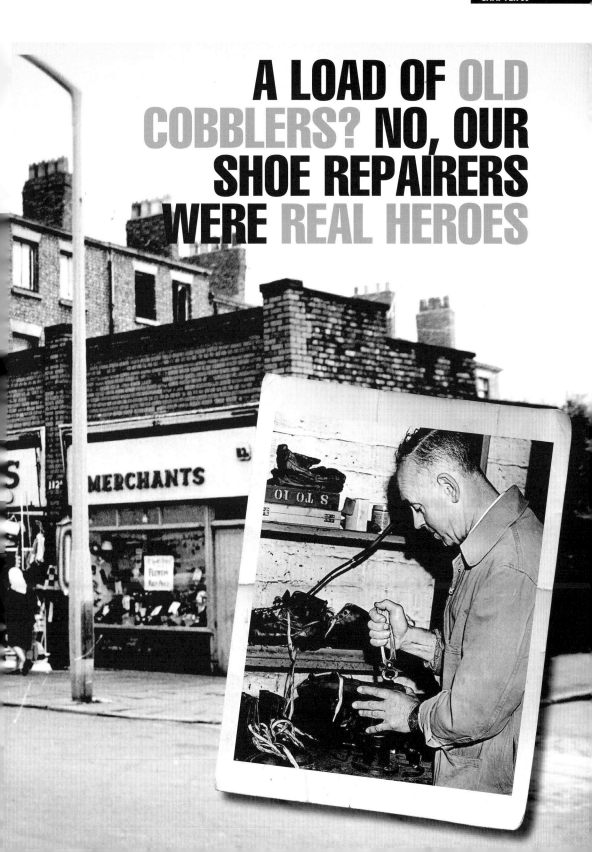

LOST TRIBE readers will have a complete understanding of the pre-1960 days when shoes were repaired several times by local cobblers before they were discarded.

I well remember a Polish cobbler on Netherfield Road North between Melbourne Street and Adelaide Street. Polish families were the exception rather than the norm in Liverpool in those days.

I often wonder what happened to that family and if they are still repairing shoes 50 years on.

Roy Hankin, formerly of Northumberland Terrace, asked me via my Liverpool Echo column if anyone remembered Fred Cooper who was a shoe repairer in Lansdowne Place.

Ray said: *"Fred was my father-in-law. If you're still waiting for your shoes, they'll be ready next Tuesday!"*

This sparked an immediate response from Glynn Hewitson who lived in Wye Street. He said: "I remember Fred Cooper quite well and also Eileen and Gary Cooper. Gary was a mate of mine when we were kids. My best memory was from Stanley Park when the fair was there.

"We were messing about and a policeman came up behind us and grabbed us by the scruff of our necks and asked our names. I told him mine and when Gary said 'Gary Cooper' the policeman gave him a whack around his head thinking he was talking about the famous Hollywood star. I still can't help chuckling about it now. Bring back those days, I say."

Kath Binnion from Winsford also responded to my column on the old cobblers. She said: *"My brother-in-law Tom Hunt is an old Everton man who lived in Abbey Street until he married my sister Betty. He was renowned for repairing the boots of the Everton football team.*

"None of these new-fangled machines. It was all done by hand with Tom holding the nails in his mouth. He was trained as a lad by William Griffiths who he remembers with pride. Tom's shop was in Green Lane, and even now he is heralded as 'Tom the cobbler' whenever he does

Shooting stars – those old fashioned footie boots

his shopping in Tuebrook. He keeps his chin up and has the old Everton spirit.

"Tom is still a strong Everton supporter and I'm sure he would still love to be cobbling away. I am very proud of him because he listened to people's cares and woes over his shop counter, and also shared their joy and happiness. Now we are hoping he can enjoy his retirement."

We will all drink to that, Kath. The traditional cobblers were crucial to every boy who had a pair of old fashioned football boots which came up to your ankles and had a solid toe cap.

Of course, they had leather soles in which the cobbler would hammer in a set of new studs whenever they became worn down. How proud we would be at the start of a new season when we could show our new studs as if the boots themselves were new. These would give us real grip on the muddy pitches that seemed to be par for the course in those days.

In the winter, you always seemed to be ankle deep in mud. Of course, the studs could get a sharp edge to them and if someone came 'foot up' into a tackle it could be really dangerous. Lucky we all wore thick pads down our socks to protect our shins. Funnily enough, down the years I witnessed a few broken ankles or legs, but not that many.

When it did occur, especially in Sunday

League games, there was always someone telling the person writhing on the floor not to worry. *"It's not broken!"*

In those situations, all the vast majority of players wanted to do was to get the injured party off the pitch so the game could continue as quickly as possible.

Whether it was a break or a really bad sprain, I have this vivid memory of the lad in excruciating pain looking up at the other 21 players with the clear instruction: *"Don't touch me!"*

Seconds later, he would be hoisted unceremoniously by several eager hands and dumped at the side of the pitch where, 20 minutes later, an ambulance would whisk him away with the game still in full flow.

This came back to haunt me when, at the age of 50 and playing in a Vets Cup game in Manchester as a guest for Liverpool Collegiate Old Boys, my ankle was broken as it twisted in a divot. Our centre-half, looking at my pained expression from 15 yards away, declared: *"It's not broken!"*

I said: *"Don't touch me."*

You can guess what happened next. But the food was nice in Manchester Royal Infirmary!

'Talking about repairing shoes and boots, the wider 'make and mend' logic was part of daily life in the old streets.

'Make and Mend', of course, was a wartime campaign to help people deal with shortages in every area of daily life.

Just a simple mention of a 'chandler's shop' brings memories flooding back of these dark and mysterious emporiums where you could buy everything from a bag of nails to a dozen coal bricks and every other conceivable household need.

The chandler's shop was one of the most important delivery mechanisms for this campaign, stocking every make of glue, every size of nail, and every tool you could imagine (and many you couldn't).

These shops seemed chaotic with their stock lines of hundreds of items seemingly scattered all over the place. But ask the manager for anything, and he would have this knack of putting his hand on it in seconds.

I have a specific memory about the chandler on St. Domingo Road in Everton where, in the 1950s, the mingling smell of candles, coal, paraffin, firelighters and firewood lives with me to this day. Strangely, these smells immediately heighten your senses and act like an odour-driven 'Time Machine', transporting you back to those old inner city districts of our youth. I can't see Dr. Who's Tardis being driven by a gallon of paraffin or by candle-power, but who needs the Time Lord when you've got a chandler's where the smells and the products combine to somehow fashion a perfect mental picture of your old granddad, who seemed to have this ability to make and mend everything under the sun?

Gill Brough (nee McNaught) contacted me on the very subject of chandlers. She said:

"My great grandfather, Alexander Hawthorn McNaught, owned three chandlers shops from about 1900-1913.

"They were situated at 361 Westminster Road, and 105 Rocky Lane, Tuebrook, with another in Granby Street. Of course, every district had at least one of these shops."

Having mentioned the chandler's on St. Domingo Road, on the opposite side, near the famous Sir Thomas White Gardens' tenements, was a builder's yard that was also crucial to the daily life of the area.

Here the lime was purchased to whitewash the thousands of drab backyard walls in the area which was an exercise that I seem to remember was fairly dangerous.

The mix used to bubble like a school chemistry experiment when water was added, so it was not to be messed with.

But a white backyard wall was almost as important as a perfectly scrubbed front step and perfectly cleaned windows.

Our parents and grandparents clearly led a simple but ordered life, and we will never forget them.

TRAM ACCIDENT AND THE RUNAWAY HORSE ON SCOTLAND ROAD

Pursued and stopped by a hero on a bike to avoid a disaster on a busy traffic route

I ALWAYS knew the people of the old inner city districts were great characters, but an 89-year-old who formerly worked in Grafton Street near the docks came up with a remarkable story about a runaway horse near Scottie Road.

Mr R.J. McCracken, who lives in Fazakerley these days, recalled: *"During the war I worked for Capstick Careful & Son, ships' engineers. I cycled to work and a tram was on the track in front of me. As I crossed behind it, I heard a loud bump. The tram had run into a horse and wagon.*

"It was in the days of the blackout and it was early morning. The wagon had a paraffin lamp hanging underneath and the tram driver just didn't see it.

"The horse bolted off, pulling the wagon, and I took off after it. I managed to overtake it towards the bottom of Byrom Street. I jumped off my bike and grabbed the horse's harness. I put my right hand on the end of the left-hand shaft and slowed the horse to an eventual halt before calming it down because it was still nervous.

"A woman came to thank me and somebody brought my bike and propped it up in the gutter. Eventually, a man in a dark blue uniform took the horse and wagon off me and I got to work on time.

"I never found out if the carter was injured. I was wondering if anyone can remember this incident. I'm 89 now, so I won't be chasing horses any more!"

What an exciting tale, reminding me of one of those cliff-hangers at the end of the old Saturday morning matinee. "Will the runaway horse get back to Scottie Road? Don't miss next week's exciting episode!"

MAYPOLE MADNESS
WOULD HAVE SENT
THE ELF & SAFETY
BRIGADE INTO A SPIN

I'm grateful I was allowed to grow up with a sense of freedom

THOSE responsible for the public parks prior to the 1960s had a very different attitude to play equipment like swings, slides and some of the more dangerous bits of metallic madness – like the Maypole.

It might sound like something a group of harmless Morris Dancers might skip around, but the Maypole, in its playground form, should have carried an X-certificate, both for those who used it and those who were inadvertently knocked off their feet or clattered in the back of the head by its flying chains.

There was a small gated playground at the top of Devonshire Place, off St. Domingo Road, which was just a couple of minutes from our house in Melbourne Street. It held a fatal fascination for me and I would cycle up there on my three-wheeler bike.

I wasn't interested in the few swings that were there. It was all about the Maypole, with its vertical central steel pole from which several chains hung down, each with a smooth wooden handle at chest height.

You would grasp this handle with both hands and start to run in a continuous circle until your feet lifted off the ground and your body stretched out into an almost horizontal position to the ground. If every chain had a kid dangling from its handle, each taking turns to run and increase the speed of the spin, it was a sight to behold. At full speed, you literally hung on for dear life.

This is when the problems started. If you tried to jump off, there was a very good chance that before you got in the clear, the lad clutching the next handle might hurtle round and knock you off your feet, or even worse, a rogue chain might hurtle round and smack you in the head.

The 'Elf & Safety' Brigade would have had a field day in some of those old playgrounds. Most had a Maypole, but your arms would start aching and you would soon have to turn your attention to the swings. Of course, a gentle up and down motion was totally unacceptable to every lad round our way.

We would jerk the swings so high that it seemed we might go right over the top in a full 360 degree loop. With the swing at maximum height, we would leap off. Obviously, the aim was to land on your feet, but the forward propulsion would usually send you tumbling onto the concrete. There were no soft landing surfaces in those days and so our park stories always ended with scuffed knees, painful ankles and sometimes a bruise on the back of the head courtesy of a Maypole chain.

What joy for young boys whose sense of adventure would take them further afield into bombed houses, or derelict old cinemas.

We did things that must seem remarkable and even reckless now in a modern world in which kids never seem to look up from their mobile, texting, or their Facebook page, and get ferried everywhere by their parents.

I'm forever grateful that I was allowed to roam around the old terraced streets and grow up with a sense of freedom and a spring in my step.

The 'debris' could be an adventure playground for little girls, as well as boys. Rubble, muck and dust did not deter these young Everton 'ladies' in the 1950s. Left, too much to choose from for this little girl in a local sweet shop

CHAPTER 33

THE SANITARY MAN WAS NEVER FAR AWAY IN THE OLD INNER CITY STREETS

Proof of overcrowding could lead to eviction and families were terrified of having the Health Department finger pointed in their direction

IN THE 19th century and into the early 20th century, Liverpool had some of the worst housing conditions in the country.

The lack of clean running water, effective sewerage and refuse disposal systems, compounded by endemic overcrowding, was a serious cause for concern.

This was particularly the case in the densely packed inner city courts (houses grouped around a narrow paved yard set at right angles to the street). There could be several courts off one road and the houses of one court would back onto the houses of another court.

The E. Chambre Hardman archive - held in what is now a National Trust Property on Rodney Street, Liverpool - reminds us that many people lived in these overcrowded courts, cellar dwellings or lodging houses. Access to a court was through a single, narrow entry from the street.

These court dwellings became places where sickness and disease spread. There was often only one water pump or tap for each court and one lavatory to be shared between the houses. A number of families would live

145

in one house and sometimes whole families would live in one room or even in a cellar.

Liverpool's first Medical Officer of Health, Dr. William Duncan (1805-1863), put together a report on this accommodation.

In it he said:

"The cellars are ten or twelve feet square; generally flagged – but frequently having only the bare earth for a floor, and sometimes less than six feet in height.

"There is frequently no window, so that light and air can gain access to the cellars only by the door, the top of which is often not higher than the level of the street . . . There is sometimes a back cellar, used as a sleeping apartment, having no direct communication with the external atmosphere, and deriving its scanty supply of light and air solely from the first apartment."

In the first edition of 'Lost Tribe' I revealed how a single word once spread fear into the hearts of the people living in the densely populated inner city districts of Liverpool, not least Everton, Scottie Road and the adjoining

Vauxhall Road area down towards the docks.

Any suggestion that the 'Nightman' might be about to pay a visit caused panic in many terraced streets, and my eldest uncle, Tom Rogers, recalled how, in the 1930s, the 'Nightman' came to visit the family's terraced house in Copeland Street, off Heyworth Street, to check for overcrowding. He gained late access to the attic and pointed a torch towards where my father was sleeping with his two brothers in a bed that was held together with string, and covered by an Army great coat.

Proof of overcrowding could lead to eviction and families were terrified of having the Health Department visit them.

Joan Murray sent me a fascinating little book written about the Sanitary Inspectors whose very presence in our former inner city districts was a clear signal that the conditions in the old terraced houses often left a lot to be desired. It is entitled: "Vanished Liverpool and the San'tree Man" – recollections of a sanitary inspector. Joan explained that the book was written by Brian Read, an inspector who operated in the Netherfield Road area of Everton in the early1950s. Joan said:

"The book highlights another facet of life in Everton as we knew it. It's a great little read and truly captures the spirit and ethos of those days, but doesn't gloss over the fact that, even in the post-war boom years of the Fifties, there were still plenty of families leading very poor lives.

"My sisters and I had a standing joke that our mother had a hot-line to the Corporation Sanitary Department. She was always sending for the Inspector to sort out blocked drains, blocked backyard toilets, plus rodent and insect invasions of all kinds.

"When our house was ultimately demolished as part of the clearances, she got a posh new flat in Sheil Park which had a panoramic view over Newsham Park. When people said 'how lovely to have such a view', she would invariably reply: 'I would sooner be back in Everton Road with my sack apron and wellies on, hose-piping the entry!' My mother passed away in 1981 aged 80 and I still think of her every day."

Many thanks for the book, Joan. Your mother's attitude just confirms the fact that communities were about the people rather than bricks and mortar. We have these fantastic memories of our old districts because of our friends and neighbours who we lost, in many cases forever, when the bulldozers rolled in.

We do have a habit of glossing over the insanitary conditions, which takes me back to Brian Read's outstanding little book, first published in 2001.

He reveals that the original title for the Sanitary Men was 'Inspector of Nuisances'. In 1950 there were about 4,000 of them employed by local authorities in Britain, so that's an awful lot of nuisance.

I was particularly interested in Brian's work because he operated in Scotland Road and also the Netherfield Ward, starting in 1951 and finishing in 1953 when I was five.

Brian recalls that the offices of the Liverpool Public Health Sanitary department were in two redundant church halls in Belmont Grove, Anfield.

It is clear that while he was confronted with difficult situations on a daily basis, he had a real respect for the people of the nearby Netherfield Ward where he pounded the steep terraced streets. He said:

"Netherfield and other areas adjoining Scotland Road were often referred to as slums. But despite the generally seedy and grimy look of the Netherfield streets of 1951 and the fact that some houses were overcrowded, it would be wrong to call the whole of Netherfield of those days a 'slum'.

"There were isolated groups of houses and individual properties, especially the 'court houses', which deserved that title, but the fact is that although many houses were in extremely poor condition and had minimal facilities (I don't think there was one house with a bathroom) most were warm and well scrubbed homes with open coal fires, comfortable furniture and a happy atmosphere.

"One could walk down most streets in the morning and see at least one kneeling woman vigorously scrubbing the sandstone step of her front door."

Clearly, Brian was one of those preaching the logic that 'cleanliness was next to godliness'. The women of Everton took this to a whole new level and they needed to because of the conditions they found themselves in.

I like Brian's book because he clearly had an astute understanding of the people and the area I was brought up in, and he is not slow to criticise those within his own department whose view was that the 'slums' – as they saw them – were not worth wasting their time and energy on.

He admits that the court houses in particular were abandoned with no efforts to improve conditions.

"Roofs leaked, floorboards were rotting, ceiling and wall plaster was either crumbling or had

disappeared," said Brian. "And yet families with children lived in these hovels and seemed to accept them with the sort of resignation that comes from never having known better."

He reveals that he visited the well-known Robsart Street where a family had complained about a leaking roof.

He was told by his manager to 'ignore them' with the following logic: "They'll all be demolished soon and the tenants rehoused."

Brian makes the point that 'soon' must have seemed a very long time to those tenants who were still there years later.

This particular 'San'tree Man' fortunately did his very best for those he visited to deal with drainage problems, leaking water pipes, obnoxious materials, and pests such as rats, mice, bed bugs, fleas, and cockroaches.

It seems hard for us to comprehend now that young children and babies were brought up in such conditions in the worst of the inner city properties.

In my first 'Lost Tribe' book I spoke about my own parents' daily battle to keep the cockroaches at bay in the 'rooms' we occupied at the time, especially in the night when they dropped down from the ceiling onto my cot.

I know, it's horrendous, but that's the way it was. However, for every problem property, many more were perfectly habitable family homes, like my grandfather's house in the Netherfield Road area that eventually became ours.

However, the Public Health department had their own unhealthy preoccupation with statistics which were used against tenants and whole districts when compulsory purchase orders were issued in those days leading up to the wholesale 'clearances' of Everton and Scotland Road.

Brian reveals:

"After my second day, I was given a form about two feet square headed: 'Monthly Summary of Inspectors Visits'. I had made ten calls the previous day so I ticked ten of the appropriate squares. This was given back to me at once.

A typical outside toilet

'What did you go to the house for?' I was asked.

"Complaint of rats," I said. 'That's one mark under the Pests Act' I was told. 'Was the roof leaking or the house in bad repair?'

"I don't think so," I said.

'Well that was an inspection under the housing acts' I was told. 'Another mark, and were there any vermin like bugs or fleas?'

"No."

'Well, that was an inspection under the verminous premises section. That's another mark.

'Was there any statutory nuisance in the house or was the house dirty?"

"No."

That's a visit under the Public Health Act. Another mark.'

And so it went on, declared Brian. It meant the total number of 'recorded visits' made by the Sanitary Department was totally misleading, but then we all know that statistics cannot lie.

And so the report for 1950 suggests that sanitary inspectors made 192,840 inspections and visits, yet the actual number of 'nuisances' reported by tenants was just 61,172.

Brian admits that this led him to distrust all statistics from bureaucratic sources.

There is no doubt that stats like this were used as one of the reasons for the total demolition of the streets of Everton from 1960 onwards.

Our street was one of them.

CHAPTER 34

EVEN THE OLD GAS LAMPS GAVE OFF MORE LIGHT THAN A MODERN ENERGY SAVING BULB

We flick the electric switch these days and take everything for granted …

Conway Street

THE European Union hastened the official demise of 'proper' light bulbs with those useless 'energy saving' alternatives now the only option unless, like half the country, you have built up a cache of the old ones to brighten up any dark evenings.

We flick the electric switch these days and take everything for granted. It scares me sometimes when I remind myself that I can actually remember the gas-only lighting systems in many of the inner city terraced houses, like that of my grandparents Tom and Emily Rogers who lived in Copeland Street.

This was back in the early 1950s when we were still using the giant re-chargeable batteries known as 'accumulators' to provide the power to play music on the old radio, something I discuss further in a later chapter.

June Woodall from Southport took this a stage further when she wrote to me about her memories of Kirkdale. She said: *"The Lamplighter would come around at dusk to light the street gas lamps. He would be on his bike and carried a long pole which he used to reach up and switch on the gas.*

"I would be swinging on the lamp, sitting on a knotted rope that was thrown over the bar across the top."

Just the mention of the word 'lamppost' is enough to get half the population of old Liverpool excited, June, let alone the entire population of 'proper' dogs that used to roam around our districts in well organised packs, having been let loose early in the morning from a thousand backyards.

Lampposts were perfect doggy 'Sat Navs' – enabling our four-legged friends to find their way home from any far flung destination. My dog, Dinky, once got back to Everton from Toxteth where he had been taken by my Uncle Bobby. That deserved a canine medal in its own right.

For every kid with a rope, lampposts were better than any fairground ride. June recalled: *"I would play for hours, just swinging round and round on my rope."*

These lampposts were instinctive meeting points for kids playing out late in the street. But back to the Lamplighter, and other key jobs confined to the history books like the 'Knocker-up' man who used to make sure you didn't sleep in and lose a vital job on the docks or in a local factory.

June concluded: *"The Lamplighter used to say the same thing every night. 'Lighten our darkness, oh Lord'.*

"I missed the Lamplighter when we went electric!"

I've been thinking, June. Those old lampposts used to give off a strange yellowy glow when it got really dark, just like these new 'energy saving' bulbs. Have we really moved on?

Above, Stanley Park open air pool.
Left, the Margaret Street baths

THE OPEN AIR BATHS ON THE DOCKS AND A CERTIFICATE FOR ONE BREADTH OF DOGGY PADDLE

The race was on to be the first one in the pool to make a splash – 'breaking the jelly'

I WAS delighted when a treasure trove of old photographs landed on my desk, highlighting the heritage around Liverpool's famous old swimming baths and wash-houses. They were rescued by 'Lost Tribe' reader Margy Boden.

We all remember where we learned to swim. I well recall having my standing leg kicked from under me in Westminster Road baths and, in the subsequent thrashing about, realising that I could keep afloat. What a moment. I've still got my one breadth certificate, earned at Major Lester School in the late Fifties doing the doggy paddle!

The photographs Margy sent me include fascinating images of Burroughs Gardens open air swimming baths, opened in 1879 in the north docks area with a purpose-built wash-house.

At that time, the inner city areas were a major poverty trap. The introduction of public baths in Liverpool was a massive step in health and cleanliness across the city.

One of the photos I was sent features the Stanley Park Open Air Pool which I well remember as a kid.

Another image highlights the historic Upper Frederick Street Baths where wash-house pioneer Kitty Wilkinson worked. She is commemorated in a stained glass window in the Anglican Cathedral.

Here is a brief history of the city's public baths and wash-houses up to 1952:

1789: Jewish community opens ritual baths - Brownlow Hill.

1794: Public Baths in Bath Street, near to current Echo building.

1816: Private floating bath launched at George's dock.

1832: Cholera epidemic. Kitty / Tom Wilkinson turn a kitchen at Denison Street into wash-house for neighbours.

1842: First Public Wash-house and Private Baths - Upper Frederick Street.

1846: Paul Street Baths and Wash-house opened.

1851: Cornwallis Street baths opened.

1860: First swimming gala in Liverpool held at Cornwallis Street. Death of Kitty Wilkinson.

1863: Margaret Street baths opened.

1874: Steble Street baths and Wash-house opened.

1877: Westminster Road baths opened.

1878: Lodge Lane Baths and Wash-house opened.

1879: Burroughs Garden baths and Wash-house opened.

1887: First Ladies' Swimming Gala held.

1895: Burlington Street free open-air bath opened.

1898: Gore Street free open-air bath opened.

1899: Green Lane free open-air bath and Mansfield Street free open-air bath and gymnasium opened.

1902: Beacon Street baths opened.

1904: Lister Drive baths opened.

1905: Springfield Street Wash-house (Old Swan) opened.

1906: Picton Road baths opened.

1907: Speke Road baths opened.

1909: Queen's Drive baths opened.

1911: Netherfield Road Wash-house opened.

1923: Stanley Park open-air bath opened.

1925: Upper Frederick Street Wash-house moved to Gilbert Street.

1927: Minshull Street Wash-house opened.

1928: Lodge Lane Wash-house modernised.

1930: Steble Street Wash-house modernised, and Melrose Road Wash-house opened.

1931: Burroughs Garden Wash-house reconstructed on new site. Solomon Street Wash-house (Kensington) opened.

1932: Liverpool Central Laundry, Burroughs Gardens, opened.

1935: Donaldson Street Wash-house and Clare Street Wash-house opened.

1936: William Roberts Baths, Norris Green, and Harold Davies Baths, Dovecot, opened.

1949: Highest total number of bathers and washers in a single year (3,248,145).

Pat Campbell from Southdene, Kirkby said: *"I was one of seven kids brought up in a house that faced the former baths in Margaret Street. We had some good times, and one of our games was waiting for it to open to try and be the first in the pool to make a splash.*

"This was known as 'breaking the jelly', disturbing the jelly-like appearance of the water. It was always an enjoyable achievement to be first in."

Pat's other memories include his mother giving him the money to pop across to Margaret Street to have a bath.

He recalls: *"We didn't have the luxury of bathrooms in those small terraced houses.*

"I suppose we had what can only be described as an outdoor en-suite, minus the bath and shower!"

An outdoor swimming pool
down near the docks

An old fruit and veg stall off Scottie Road.
Above, a large family gather for this photo
of Scarlet Street in 1933

CHAPTER 36

THE LONGEST NAME EVER GIVEN ON AN INNER CITY BIRTH CERTIFICATE

In 1882, laundryman Arthur Pepper and his wife celebrated the birth of a daughter – her forenames used every letter of the alphabet!

WHEN I wrote in the Liverpool Echo about unusual names in the old inner city districts – like Enoch Tart and Gertrude Mangies – it brought a superb response from Joan Murray.

She said: *"We lived in Everton Road on the corner of Bright Street and had a neighbour who sold fruit and veg from his pony and cart. He was Mickey Jinks. His wife was Minny Jinks. Mickey and Minnie Jinks sounds like a cinema cartoon, doesn't it? They were a nice and decent family though."*

Great names Joan, but mention of the word 'Jinks' revives different memories for me. In the early Seventies, I was one of two lead singers in a group called *Hurles Jinx*, having started with another group called 'The Circulation'.

These groups played in all of the city centre clubs like The Mardi Gras, Victoriana, Peppermint Lounge, Blue Angel, Beachcomber, and Cavern. Other venues included the Litherland Town Hall where The Beatles played loads of times.

Contemporaries at that time included *Colonel Bagshot's* who had set the trend for two lead singers. One of them was Mike

REGISTRATION DISTRICT					WEST DERBY				

1883 BIRTH in the Sub-district of **West Derby Rural**   in the   County of Lancaster

Columns:-	1	2	3	4	5	6	7	8	9	10
No.	When and where born	Name, if any	Sex	Name and surname of father	Name, surname and maiden surname of mother	Occupation of father	Signature, description and residence of informant	When registered	Signature of registrar	Name entered after registration
153	Nineteenth December 1882 204a West Derby Road	Anna Bertha Cecilia Diana Emily Fanny Gertrude Hypatia Inez Jane Kate Louisa Maud Nora Ophelia Quince Rebecca Starkey Teresa Ulysis Venus Winifred Xenephon Yetty Zeus	Girl	Arthur Pepper	Sarah Jane Pepper formerly Creighton	Laundry man	Arthur Pepper Father 204a West Derby Road West Derby	Eighth January 1883	J. Hunter Registrar	

Byrne, one of the inspirations behind the Beatles Story Museum on the Albert Dock when it opened in 1990.

Mike has had a great musical career and is still performing. His group, which had the additional tag of the *Amazing Bucket Band,* were first class. I would like to think we had some ability to have played in clubs like the Cavern, but it was the name that intrigued people. *Hurles Jinx!*

Of course, every inner city kid from the Fifties will know that *Jinx* were coloured beer bottle tops. We used them in a game that was a spin on Pitch and Toss. Nearest to the wall would win. Hence, I often had hundreds of beer bottle tops in a proud collection, matched only by my cache of ollies. Perhaps ultimately joining a group called *Hurles Jinx* was inevitable.

Instead of buying your young grandson a new mobile phone this Christmas, an iPad or an X-Box computer, why not suggest a bag of jinx, or a jar of marbles and let me know the response!

But back to Joan Murray's letter about unusual names. Joan, a fellow Everton historian, reminded me of a newspaper cutting she discovered highlighting the longest name given to a Liverpool child.

On December 13, 1882, laundryman Arthur Pepper and his wife Sarah Jane from 204a West Derby Road celebrated the birth of a daughter (see birth certificate above).

They named her: *Anna Bertha Cecelia Diana Emily Fanny Gertrude Hypatia Inez Jane Kate Louisa Maud Nora Orphelia Quince Rebbeca Starkey Teresa Ulysis Venus Winifred Xenephon Yetty Zeus Pepper,* or Alpha Pepper for short! Her forenames used every letter of the alphabet.

'P' was omitted because it was already in her surname.

Joan said:

"We knew the descendants of the Peppers. They had a Brunswick Road herbal shop. Pat Pepper was my age and Alpha's granddaughter. They all left the district during the 1960s clearances, just as we did."

Teenage dreams for these lads on the steps of Shrewsbury House Youth Centre in Everton

St. Domingo Road, 1961, and (below) the famous pub
at the junction of Everton Valley and Walton Road

Elephants from Billy Smart's Circus
parade through Liverpool in 1959

CHAPTER 37

AN ELEPHANT, A LION, AND LLAMAS ON THE STREETS OF EVERTON

A wild tale of things that go bump in the night . . .

I KNOW the inner city streets were always a walk on the wild side, but a memory left on my *Lost Tribe of Everton* website managed to take this to a whole new level.

Chris Evans' family lived in the famous Roscommon Street in Everton, and later Heyworth Street. He said:

"We lived next to Roscommon Street School at number 81. My dad, also Chris, had a family haulage business. This included stables which occupied number 79, so our full postal address was 79/81 Roscommon Street. How posh is that! Not really.

"My mam worked as a night nurse and my dad let out parts of the stables just to stay afloat. The rent on the premises seemed a constant struggle. A bonus from this was that I grew up, with my brothers Les and Ron, amongst horses, goats, llamas, elephants – and for one night only – a lion!"

Now come on, Chris. Are you telling me that a real lion was holed up in the heart of one of our most densely populated inner city areas?

I've highlighted that the famous explorer Sir Henry Morton Stanley once lived close to Roscommon Street before he set off for Africa to find the legendary Dr. David Livingstone in 1871. Indeed, my school 'house' at Evered

High in Walton was called Stanley. But a lion in Everton? Chris confirmed:

"The lion incident did happen! For one night it was in a cage on the back of a lorry, parked in front of number 83 Roscommon Street with a sheet covering it. The lion kept everyone awake and wouldn't settle. There were so many complaints that my dad told the owners of the circus that it couldn't stay another night."

Chris added:

"These animals mainly belonged to the circuses of Billy Smart or Chipperfield, but our stables also provided hostelry for the pantomime season animals, including Shetland ponies and mules.

"I recall a young Ken Dodd playing Buttons in Cinderella making his entrance on a Jack Ass at the Empire Theatre. Cinderella's coach was pulled by four Shetland ponies that we had helped groom and feed that day. We even stabled an elephant in the front 'loose box' once and he managed to lift the roof and break out. He was free overnight before being found.

"The front yard where we kept the lorries went from 79 to 83. It must have been inconvenient to No. 83's residents as the working day started at 6am and could extend into the night.

"On a winter's morning, the sound of lorries being cold started, constantly revving their engines, could be quite horrendous.

"In 1961 we moved to 69 Heyworth Street as the demolition process began, keeping the stables and yard for the transport business.

"Sadly, my dad and mam got divorced when we lived in Heyworth Street. It would be nice to hear from anyone who remembers the stables and the animals trekking to the circus through the streets of Everton, or memories of our sweetshop next to Heyworth Street School."

I had an immediate response to Chris's remarkable story which did not so much surprise June Woodall as delight her, because it ratified a tall story her husband always told her from the 1950s. June said:

"My husband came home one night after having a drink in the city centre Basnett Bar (a wonderful pub I might add). When he came out

at closing time (10.30 in those days) thick smog had come down. He didn't own a car then and the trams and buses were off so he began to walk home.

"When he reached Low Hill, shortly before you get to Kensington, he saw two elephants approaching with their keeper out of the fog. He said they didn't make a sound, just the whoosh, whoosh of their feet as they went on their way.

"Needless to say, my husband took a lot of stick every time he told that tale. But reading this, they were obviously going back to the stables owned by Chris's father."

Chris was delighted with June's memory. He said:

"It's good to know after all these years that someone actually witnessed the elephants. I'm surprised there weren't more as the elephants were also taken via the side streets to Stanley Park and Walton Park in the daytime."

We've all got these stories which tend to get embellished down the years and become so distant in our memories that we begin to wonder if they actually happened, so I can understand Chris's delight at June's confirmation of the elephants' story.

In my 'Lost Tribe of Everton & Scottie Road' book I recalled a day in the Fifties when a Covered Wagon rolled along Netherfield

Road pulled by a team of horses, surrounded by several Cowboys and Indians on horseback!

It turned out to be a highly effective early marketing promotion for Wagon Wheel biscuits.

That didn't worry me. I was straight into our house in Melbourne Street to don my cowboy suit and was soon back on the streets with my two six shooters in their holsters in search of that covered wagon. I had it in mind that they might take me back to the prairies with them where I would meet my hero Roy Rogers.

Years later, I was actually in the States, heading on a coach from Los Angeles to Las Vegas, when I suddenly spotted the Roy Rogers Museum as we sped through Victorsville. I nearly caused the bus to come off the road with my scream of excitement.

Unfortunately, the coach sped on and I never got to see my hero's remarkable collection of memorabilia, including his stuffed and mounted horse Trigger (my second greatest hero of all time). The museum was closed in 2007 and everything was sold for £2.9 million. At least I've got my memories!

Chris gave it another twist when he said:

"Your cowboy hero was Roy Rogers and it reminded me of the visit of the Lone Ranger (Clayton Moore) to Lewis's store in Liverpool city centre at that time. Unlike yourself, I always played an Indian, and was disappointed that Tonto (Jay Silverheels) was not there. I got a signed photograph of Tonto and 'Kemo Sabi' (Tonto's Indian name for his masked partner) from Beverley Hills, California, that Christmas.

"Who was that man? For me it really was the Lone Ranger! Happy Trails."

There is a punchline to the story about the Roscommon Street stables, temporary home to so many unusual animals. Liz Woodbridge made contact via the 'Lost Tribe' website to give the story even more depth by taking it back a further generation.

She recalled:

"The original Evans' stables were in Comus Street off Scotland Road. My uncle, Charlie Evans, owned them and he was well known in the haulage business before and after the war.

"He was a good friend of Rob Wilton, the famous Liverpool comedian who often referred to 'my friend Charlie Evans' in his patter.

"When the circus was in town, often appearing at the Shakespeare Theatre, the animals paraded along the streets, led by Saucy and Salty, the world famous elephants. When they reached the gates of the stables in Comus Street the elephants often reared up on their hind legs and trumpeted to announce their arrival.

"Me and my Auntie Jane often greeted them at the gates with buns. On one occasion, when I was a little girl, one of the elephants lifted me high into the air with its trunk and carefully placed me on its back. This is an experience I have never forgotten in 65 years!

"The stables were huge, on two levels, and were able to accommodate all the animals including horses and even lions in cages. The stables are no more, having sadly disappeared in the Sixties clearances. Chris Evans Snr. from Roscommon Street was one of Charlie Evans' sons."

So there you have it. Life in Everton was definitely a walk on the wild side!

CHAPTER 38

COMIC DAYS WHEN THE HOTSPUR STIRRED THE BOYS AND THE BUNTY INSPIRED THE GIRLS

And radiograms were powered by batteries as large as a modern telly!

COMPUTER games play a huge part in the life of today's youngsters.

Modern technology is truly remarkable, transporting kids into a cyber world that is beyond comprehension for many people whose adventure heroes were all confined to the pages of those classic comics of the Forties, Fifties and Sixties.

Bert Hamblet from Meols reminded me of this when he recalled how these publications built up into treasured collections. He said:

"I was born in 1935 and lived off Belmont Road next to the old Barker & Dobson factory.

"When I was 12, in 1947, a friend at school told me that a cobbler's shop by him had pre-war comics for sale at a penny each. They were called 'The Magnet' and featured the exploits of Billy Bunter at Greyfriars School.

"Each day, after leaving my own All Saints School on Oakfield Road, I would go up to that cobbler in Lance Street and buy three or four comics. At the end of six months, I must have had over 300. Then the well ran dry, the comics stopped, and my mother told me to get rid of them because the house smelled like a second hand junk shop.

Three young barefoot boys sit on the steps of St. George's Hall in the early part of the last century 'reading' an edition of the old broadsheet Liverpool Echo. Of course, their only priority would have been survival and many youngsters of this age could neither read nor write at this time

"There was another source in Breck Road called Humphreys OK Bookshop. They would sell pre-war film books and comics such as Picturegoer, Picture Show, Picture Post, Rover, Wizard, Hotspur, Adventure, and Champion. Instead of a penny or tuppence, they would charge sixpence each."

You've started something now, Bert. You mentioned Hotspur which I bought every week with my paper round money.

I also bought a part-work encyclopaedia at that time called 'Knowledge' and I still have the two binders with their colourful magazines inside after all these years. Hotspur was story-driven, rather than pictures, and was published until 1959.

There was also The Wizard and I remember Tiger Magazine, and don't get me started on the Dandy (Korky the Cat, and Desperate Dan) and the Beano (Dennis the Menace, and the Bash Street Kids). You will all remember the larger format Topper with its Mickey the Monkey comic strip on the front page.

Of course, the Eagle was a different class with its high quality colour printing and tales of my very own super hero Dan Dare. In the office, I used to bang on so much about the Dan Dare Space Station I had as a kid, that the staff went on eBay and bought me one for a recent birthday. It was like Christmas 1958 all over again!

Alright ladies, I'm not forgetting your passion for comics like Bunty, Jackie, Judy, Jinty and later, Tammy. Some of these titles might have been pure entertainment with not a lot of literary depth, but the most important thing is that they got us reading and kept us reading.

You should never read Shakespeare without first reading Korky the Cat.

'Korky, Korky, wherefore art thou, Korky?'

In the Dandy, of course, and in its own way, as important as any classic ever written!

Life as we all remember it, was clearly very different for the kids of the old inner city terraced streets of Liverpool. James Maher, who was brought up in Sim Street, spoke for all of us when he reflected how we benefited, not from computers, but from the simple fact that we had the space in the streets to play and express ourselves, simply because there were very few cars to interrupt the street games before the 1960s. James wrote:

"It was amazing to see neighbours jumping into the youngsters' skipping ropes and some of the older 'skippers' were real experts.

"They could skip in two ropes (that whirled in opposite directions).

I wonder if your readers remember putting wet 'Nutty Slack' on the open fires. The room would be full of smoke, but the fire would last longer.

"Then we had the 'Knocker Upper', whose job would be to go round the streets very early in the morning, tapping on the windows to wake up the workers. You would be getting ready for school and looking for your shirt, only to be told your dad had to wear it for work. Then you would be sent on a message for one of the neighbours.

"On getting back, you would use your free hand to knock on the door, and drop a full bottle of milk! The doors were not always open, as legend has it.

"I can remember going to a shop on Kirkdale Road to change the accumulator to charge up the radio (which highlights how many houses lacked electricity, even in the 1950s). I dropped one once, only to be told it was full of acid! The lack of electricity meant many houses had gaslights. We would be sent for a new gas mantle (the end bit that provided the illumination). They came loose or in a little cardboard box. They were so fragile you rarely made it home with the mantle intact.

"We had our shoes until they were worn out, and then put cardboard inside to cover the holes. I still do it now (ha, ha!). What saved the day was when the revolutionary stick on rubber soles came out!"

James' memories would bring a shrug of total disbelief from today's high tech generation, but it's worth remembering that it's all within our lifetime. I wonder, James, if one of those giant old accumulators would drive a modern 48 inch 3-D television?

Possibly, but it wouldn't be worth it if the only signal being picked up delivered nothing but the old black and white 'B' movies!

On the question of accumulators, Mrs. Evans (nee Henderson) wrote to me to say: *"The accumulator shop mentioned in Kirkdale Road was run by John Bennett who later moved to Walton Road.*

"I still see John now and again. What a great man. I remember when we got our first

A family gather to watch television in the 1950s

radiogram. We would have been lost without the accumulators from shops like John's."

That's absolutely correct. I can also remember going down to Kirkdale Road with my parents to collect an accumulator to power up my granddad's old radiogram, a combined record player and radio in a polished wood case that was more like a piece of furniture than a statement of technology.

Of course, it was high-tech in its day in the early 1950s. I'd love to have it now, if only to look at the names of the old radio stations on the large round dial, like Athlone, Luxembourg, Hilversum, Budapest, Lille, and Allouise. You would get that high pitched signal that would ebb and flow as you crossed the world with one turn of the wrist.

Without electricity in those old terraced houses, the accumulator was crucial. When the power ran out, you simply returned it to the shop, swopping it for a fully charged alternative. The only snag was that these accumulators were large and heavy.

You needed an old pram to transport them, especially up those steep Everton streets.

The radio was still king in the early 1950s when very few people around our way had televisions. We all tuned in to classic shows like The Goons, and Hancock's Half Hour.

Whatever happened to my granddad's old radiogram? It probably went onto a November 5th bonfire circa 1958, usurped by a bright red Dansette record player!

Ellison Street, off Netherfield Road North

THE 'BOOKIES RUNNERS' WHO WERE ALWAYS ONE STEP AHEAD OF THE LOCAL 'BOBBY' ON THE BEAT

Bare faced cheek of the chancers — but my luck ran out in Belmont Road Hospital

EVEN though I was Sports Editor of the Liverpool Echo for a decade, I've never been a great sports gambler. Like most people, I am usually only tempted occasionally by major events like the Grand National and even then it's selecting by colours or instinctive names.

However, I was always fascinated as a kid by those bookies runners who would hang around on inner city street corners or on debris areas, trying to keep a low profile from any 'Bobby' on the beat while making themselves available to those who fancied a flutter on the horses.

In 1961, Harold Macmillan's Conservative Government finally legalised betting shops and those old street corner characters began to disappear, although they seemed to hold their own in the big factories. Some of the 8,500 betting shops in the UK these days tempt customers with free tea and coffee and streamlined high tech facilities. You can bet on just about anything now.

However, the early shops were not like that. Pat Goldstein (Skelly) from Everton worked in O'Connors on Heyworth Street around 1969.

She says: *"There were no TV screens then, just Ted the boardmarker. He was a lovely man and used to call me 'Missy'.*

"Peggy Murphy, the settler of bets, was great. A character called Frank used to come in every morning when it was cold outside (as well as in!). There were no heaters then, only a one bar electric fire over the door. I used to fill up Frank's tin caddy with hot water. Then he would give me a song, usually something by Mario Lanza. What a marvellous voice he had. He was a scruffy unshaven fella, but he had probably been quite handsome.

"A young David Johnson, later to play for Everton and Liverpool, would sometimes pop in. I went on to work for several betting shops over seven years and also became manageress of the Crown Pub in Norris Green, but it's those lovely care-free days on Heyworth Street that I remember most."

Pat, I've got this incredible visual picture in my mind of your 'Mario Lanza' character hitting those high notes. He'd probably be a prime candidate for the X-Factor these days.

A close shave in the kitchen

An evening in for husband and wife in the 1950s

And I can also remember that day sometime in the 1950s when my mother invested in a three-bar Magicoal electric fire for the kitchen in Melbourne Street.

One less use for the Liverpool Echo without which the old open fires could never have been lit! The light bulb behind the fake plastic coal would give off a golden glow, but it was never the same as coming in from school to be greeted by that roaring open fire, exuding that special warmth that made everything right with the world.

We have all come through a series of revolutions in our lives, and I'm not talking about wars or civil unrest. I often smile looking back because day to day living has been turned on its head over the past 50 years.

Many of the people reading this book will clearly remember a time when most people did not have a television or viewed a small 14 inch screen in flickering black and white. Likewise, telephones were the exception rather than the rule and the age of the mobile phone was a sci-fi dream.

I can remember a time in the Fifties when we didn't have a single car in our street. This inspired a street games culture for youngsters that we do not see today. And then we had all of those bizarre rituals that seem almost prehistoric now.

In one of my Liverpool Echo 'Lost Tribes' columns, Pat Campbell from Southdene, Kirkby, mentioned about people cleaning their

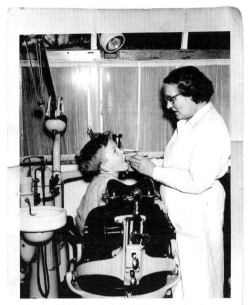

'Open wide' – the dreaded visit to the dentist

teeth using chimney soot from the open fires, or even using salt.

Pat said:

"One of my older sisters informed me that she can recall using a mixture of salt and soot to clean her teeth, using her finger as a toothbrush.

"It would be interesting to know if any other readers used this strange way of cleaning their teeth."

I have to admit to doing this myself at least once in the 1950s, Pat, and all I can say is thank God, for modern toothpaste.

Kath Binnion of Winsford wrote to me to say:

"I was part of the soot and salt brigade. Needless to say it was mostly salt until one Christmas my elder sister Joan bought me a tin of Gibbs toothpaste. It was in a round tin and was a gift I treasured. Joan also used to wash my hair in green spirit soap. It didn't smell very nice, but boy did it make your hair shine.

"I think back now and remember Belmont Road Hospital which, years before, had been used as an old workhouse. In my youth, the hospital was used for the treatment of skin problems such as scabies. They would put you in a bath and paint you with purple lotion. I was one of the unlucky ones who had to go for treatment and suffer the indignity. It was a good job I was only a kid."

I shudder at the very mention of the words Belmont Road Hospital. Kath has reminded me of my most embarrassing moment as a teenager. I went to that hospital because I had developed a rash on my arm and was pointed into a cubicle and told by a busy nurse to take my clothes off. There was one door into the cubicle and then another one directly opposite.

Suddenly there was a knock on this second door and a voice said: "Come in". I thought I was going into the doctor's room but stepped out into a much larger consultation area where the Consultant was waiting with a pack of young medical students. The nurse had forgotten to give me a gown and there I was, standing there in the raw, with my face a damn sight redder than the small rash on my arm. It was like a scene from a 'Carry On' film.

I expected 'Matron' in the shape of the large and domineering Hattie Jacques to come blustering in through the door clutching my robe. As it turned out, there was no sign of her, Kenneth Williams, Kenneth Connor, or Charles Hawtrey, but I swear one of those students gave a perfect impression of Sid James' dirty laugh!

Needless to say, just a mention of Belmont Road Hospital makes me cringe now!

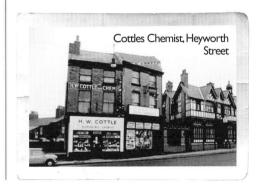

Cottles Chemist, Heyworth Street

WAS THE DESTRUCTION OF EVERTON AND SCOTTIE A MASSIVE ERROR OF JUDGEMENT BY THE PLANNERS?

I TRUST you have revelled in the memories articulated with such passion and no shortage of humour in the previous chapters by the proud and passionate members of 'Lost Tribe of Everton & Scottie Road'

Your stories have been inspirational, remarkable, packed full of humour and surprise, even heartbreaking at times. But in my mind, one thing comes across loud and clear.

You speak with one voice. It's as if you all come from the same group, the same family, dare I say it, the same TRIBE.

It makes me once again pose an intriguing question:

Was the 1960s slum clearance programme that virtually wiped the famous and historic districts of Everton and Scotland Road off the inner city map of Liverpool a massive error of judgment by the politicians and the planners of the day? Was mass exodus the only solution?

Was there a more radical and visionary solution, or part solution, staring the politicians and planners in the face?

CHAPTER 40

MP Bessie Braddock on a
visit to Everton in 1962

I've no doubt that the local politicians, driven by the right motives, believed that slum clearance was a policy to be achieved at any cost. But what was driving their logic in the Town Hall? Did anyone ever stand up in a Council meeting and ask what the people they were representing truly wanted, or was there an attitude of 'The buildings must go, so the vast majority of the people must go too?

How were the pros and cons of mass slum clearance discussed and debated? Did any planning officer or councillor have a simple flip chart featuring two separate columns under the headers: 'Case for mass demolition' and 'Cause for concern'?

Let's think about that potential chart now.

The demolition of Sir Thomas White Gardens

PLUSES FOR MASS DEMOLITION:	CAUSE FOR CONCERN:
■ Housing stock in a desperate state	■ The people, the community,
■ Cramped conditions way above the national average	■ Friends and neighbours
■ Potential in such conditions for the spread of disease	
■ Properties damp and past their sell-by date	
■ Vermin issues i.e. rats, mice, cockroaches	
■ Lack of basic services	
■ No inside toilets (or very few)	
■ No hot running water	
■ No bathrooms	
■ Concrete jungle, no green spaces	
■ Massive waiting list for houses	

Okay, in a few seconds I've made a powerful case for those decision-makers who only saw one solution.

At the same time, I may appear to have under-played things in the **'Cause for concern'** column – or have I?

You see, I believe those seven simple words in column two are not just hugely important. **THEY ARE ALL IMPORTANT.** *They are not meant to question or dispute any of the points made in column one.*

Indeed, I'm happy to put a huge tick alongside everything in the 'case for mass demolition' line. Yet every time I drive down Vauxhall Road these days and look across the Leeds-Liverpool Canal towards the remarkable and world-class community success story that is the Eldonian Village, it raises a tantalising and frustrating thought in my mind.

Was the bulldozing of Everton and Scottie Road an absolute no-brainer because of the state of the housing stock and that list of outlined negatives, or was there actually a more radical and visionary solution, or part solution, staring the politicians and the planners in the face? I'm not going to try and answer that question myself.

I'm going to put it to a man who has always stood shoulder to shoulder with: the people; the community; relatives; friends and neighbours.

For over 30 years, Tony McGann has been the heartbeat and the inspiration behind the development of the Eldonian Village project that I referred to at the start of this chapter (with a little help from his friends, of course, of whom there are many).

He fully understands what previously happened in 'Scottie' and further up the hill because his family were caught up in the original 'clearances'.

Tony, one of ten children, was born and brought up in Gildarts Gardens, old 'court style' properties built in 1897.

"There were ten of us in two rooms," recalled Tony. *"I think they stacked us on pallet boards to get us in there. But everyone was in the same boat."*

Between 1968 and 1971, these dwellings and many others, including 500 houses that had been built just five years earlier, would ultimately disappear into the biggest hole in the ground ever dug in Liverpool before or since.

I'm talking about that soulless sweep of curving road that serves as the entrance to the Kingsway Mersey Tunnel, or as we still call it over 40 years on: 'the new tunnel'.

Tony recalls:

"Where I lived was right on top of that tunnel site. All the housing around us got demolished. No consultation, no nothing. Thousands of jobs and hundreds of little companies also went down that hole in the ground. People were just scattered to the four winds.

"But part of the community was still left, and I moved along to Burlington Street in the five-storey blocks."

Throughout the Sixties and into the

Seventies, people had been shipped out in their mega thousands to new towns on the outskirts of the city. Strong communities continued to be broken up and this had a profound effect on Tony.

He told me:

"I was born and bred in the Scotland Road area where the people have always been close. I left school at 15 in 1951. I finished at twelve o' clock and an hour later I was working in a local cooperage. Jobs were plentiful then and while they paid buttons, the people were wonderful. We had nothing, but what we had we shared."

After the disappearance of Gildarts Gardens, Tony moved with his family into a flat in Burlington Street. He said:

"I was lucky to get one of those. Old neighbours wanted to be kept together. The Tate & Lyle sugar refinery was close. The British American Tobacco Factory was close. The Docks were close.

"But having moved into Burlington Street with my family, the council then decided they were going to demolish all of the flats in that area as well. The people were distraught. They had seen what had happened before (on Scottie Road and across the district of Everton). They did not want to move or be separated. They wanted new houses and they wanted them in the area they were living in."

In the years he lived in Burlington Street, Tony had become a point of community contact and support for people who had issues around housing, repairs, maintenance and even rent arrears. He was known as someone who could get things done, working closely with local councillor Paul Orr.

In 1978, when the City Council announced its plans to demolish the tenements in the Vauxhall Road area, notably those around Burlington and Eldon Streets, Tony began to formulate his thoughts about a radical alternative to the council's policy of knocking houses down, clearing sites and sweeping people to all corners of the city. Local planners had no real strategy for keeping neighbourhoods together and moving them as a community group. Tony explained:

"The people were confused and frightened about what might happen to them. We had a meeting and the simple message was that we were not moving. The answer was to fight back and so we set up the Eldonian Consultation Committee. We did not want the community broken up.

"People spoke about the Radcliffe Estate up the hill in Everton. It had been a new build, but the planners did not involve the local people and so it had major problems. We said: 'This is about our lives. This is why you must talk to us.'"

However, the defiant stance of the 'Eldonians' was complicated by the political situation in Liverpool City Council at that time. Between 1973 and 1983, no party had an overall majority.

Tony and the 'Eldonians' still pressed on and a meeting was called, attended by over 250 people, including the supportive local priest from Our Lady's, Eldon Street, Jim Dunne. The local councillors did not understand the level of community frustration and felt that their job at that meeting was to talk about improving the city and improving the lot of the people by demolishing the poor housing.

The priest stepped forward and, as silence finally descended on the room, said to the councillors:

"Who gave you the authority to say that these tenements should come down?"

Suddenly the people were on the front foot and demanding to know why they had to move from the area their families had lived in for generations. Tony recalls:

"Paul Orr suggested we do a survey about the residents' views to present to the Council. This was the first time we'd been asked what we wanted.

"Ordinary men and women, helped by the priest, quickly got on with the survey and it showed that 90 per cent did not want to move.

"It was clear the people wanted more control, so the battle was on."

There was an acceptance that the tenements needed demolishing, but there was now clarity that the community was determined to stay together. In the early 1980s, the Eldonian Community Association was formed. It used the name of the famous old street where Our Lady's Roman Catholic Church still stands at the heart of the community. Tony was elected chairman.

It was still extremely difficult dealing with the Council, but this only increased the determination of the people to be re-housed locally, rather than be transported into available properties on the outer limits of the city.

However, three of the main reasons for staying in the area were no longer positives. Tony said: *"Some people were now saying 'What do you want to live round here for? Tate's is going. B.A.T. is going. The docks are going.'*

"We said that we didn't care. We would get the housing right and then get the jobs right."

One of the things highlighted by the residents' survey was that Portland Gardens was in a worse state than the Eldon and Burlington Street tenements, so this got priority.

The Council agreed that Portland Gardens would be the first priority and the plan was to reduce them from four storeys high to two, effectively creating two-storey terraced properties. One of the blocks would become sheltered accommodation for the elderly.

Portland Gardens

Gildarts Gardens in 1965

George Evans now came into the picture, a man from the Council's Housing Department who would later find himself on the other side of the fence as Chief Executive of the Eldonians. At that time, George's job was to deal with the short term re-housing of the Portland Gardens residents while the redevelopment of those properties went on.

This really is the nub of any 'clearance' programme. How do you solve the short term fix?

George explained:

"When someone from the Burlington Street tenements had accepted an offer to move to another part of the city and they moved house on the Friday, Tony and I would know someone in Portland Gardens who would move temporarily so that we could free up the Portland Gardens property and ultimately the block to enable them to be demolished/refurbished more quickly."

It took 18 months for the initial 112 families to be temporarily re-housed, highlighting that this was no quick fix. However, it was more about the long game as far as the community was concerned.

There is an outstanding book entitled 'The rebirth of Liverpool – the Eldonian way' by Jack McBane that covers in detail the journey of those Vauxhall residents from humble beginnings to the remarkable project that is still going from strength to strength today.

If you became a member of the 'Lost Tribe of Everton & Scottie Road' I would recommend you try to read it because it sums up how things might have been so different in our old district instead of the High Rise disaster and the mass exodus to the suburbs that changed the face of the former Liverpool 5 forever.

However, in the next chapter I will explain how the 'Eldonians' had to come through a series of hurdles and obstacles with steely determination to achieve their dreams.

They feared the new era of the militant tendency in Liverpool would threaten everything they had been working towards.

It was at this point that a crucial decision was taken by the locals. Did they want to be re-housed out of the area by the Council?

Did they want to stay within the area but remain as council tenants?

Or did they want to consider the bold new idea of joint ownership and management by the residents, in other words a Housing Co-operative? Even though there was less clarity about the latter, 112 families from Portland Gardens decided on this option.

The most important thing here was the word 'option' which immediately took me back to the early 1960s when the people along Netherfield Road where I lived were given ultimatums rather than options.

The threat was that you would get three housing offers from the council and if you didn't feel that any of them was right, for whatever reason, you could be taken off the housing list. This 'three strikes and you're out' rule terrified many people and forced rash decisions.

Now, down in the Vauxhall Road area, there wasn't just choice, but an option for friends, neighbours and relatives to stay together. At least, this seemed to be the case.

The only place to play
with a bit of adventure
– the old Eldon Grove
tenements in April 1972

U-TURN BY MILITANTS ON THE COUNCIL THAT THREATENED ELDONIAN DREAMS OF A FUTURE TOGETHER

The people were now motivated and mobilised — the Eldonians had to go to war to fulfil their dreams

DIRECT action by the Eldonians, when it was needed, would become part of their strategy, but they knew that the real route to press forward was by further exploring their housing cooperative options, not least because they now needed dramatically more houses.

Two associations were fostering cooperatives and in 1982 the Eldonians contacted Merseyside Improved Housing (MIH).

Jack McBane was one of the people at MIH who gave outstanding advice, with continued support coming from Councillor Paul Orr.

One major problem was that there was only space for 51 houses on the sites they had identified for potential redevelopment. Rather than think small, the Eldonians now decided to think big, widening their remit to 'take up the housing challenge for the whole neighbourhood'.

In 1982, the Portland Gardens Housing Cooperative had been formed with the late Billy Little as its chairman, an astute and determined campaigner. The wider Community Association was going from strength to strength and an exhibition would now highlight the aims of the Eldonians under the banner: 'We'll do a better job ourselves'.

The people were now motivated and mobilised. By May 1983, designs were on the board and new houses had at last been allocated to each of the 112 Portland Gardens families.

However, an election bombshell now threatened to derail the future plans of the Eldonians.

News broke that the Labour Party had won an overall majority on the Council and their strategy was about large council owned housing estates, not cooperatives.

Indeed, within days, the Labour council declared they were not interested in tenant participation schemes and it was clear they were not interested in any commitments made by the previous Liberal administration. It took a judicial review to over-turn that one.

Tony McGann was clearly a Labour man through and through, but the arrival of the flamboyant and single-minded Derek Hatton on the local Council scene was now threatening to turn all of the hopes and dreams of the Eldonians upside down.

Tony explained:
"The Militants immediately got their feet under the table and they said that Housing Cooperatives were elitist. Elitist? People were living in a load of crap here. 'We're going to municipalise them' the Militants said.

"We thought: 'This is the first time our people have got a say in their own life.' They've got a say in their destiny. But the Militants didn't see it that way.

"If things moved forward the way we wanted, we would own the land our houses were being built on. We had plans to build 1,000 new homes in three years, although that was optimistic. Now we were suddenly having our status removed, along with six other 'cooperatives'.

"Of course, there were all kinds of demonstrations. I used to get ripped to pieces down at the council meetings. At least the

Portland Gardens development was keeping some of our plans on the table, but as soon as the first eleven houses were built, the Militants moved the goalposts again.

"They were now saying that single people would not be getting any of those houses, people who had been three to four years in the planning. They said that these individuals could go into the High Rise blocks, which meant pensioners as well."

This was not what it was all about for Tony and the Eldonians. He recalls:
"On the day those first eleven people were due to move in, the council came down and said: 'That house is going to another man because he has had heart trouble'.

"I said: 'The old woman who was going in there will have a broken heart!'

"We had to take action and the next day we moved that lady in with all of her furniture. We barricaded the house, squatted and even brought in Alsatian dogs for protection. When the bailiffs came, we chased them.

"In the meantime the big site we had was on Latimer Street with 67 houses. So the council said: 'Make sure you get all the guards on site because the Eldonians will pull a stroke down there. Make sure they don't get near this site, or they'll start doing what they did with the other person.

"One of our lads, Billy Little, got all dressed up, and carried a camera and a notepad. Billy turned up and said: 'I'm from such-and-such magazine. Can I come and take some photographs of this co-op?'

"They said 'yeah go on in there' and bang! We took the rest of the building. We had them running round in circles.

"While we were doing this it gave us the time for the judicial review to go through. All the people who were designated for those houses got them, even though they were council.

"You couldn't have planned that one!"

The loss of the Tate & Lyle business had been catastrophic for the local community when it had happened in 1981.

Tony said:

"All the people round here lost their jobs at that time. They had an excellent workforce at Tate's, but they were just thrown on the scrap-heap when Tate's decided to go down to London."

But the Eldonians had retained their focus and were now considering the possibilities that the vacant land had opened up.

Tony knew that if they could get that site, the Eldonians could move forward again with real momentum to help even more families.

He explained:

"Tate's appeared to own the land, but the responsibility for its development was with English Estate. We now went to the people of Burlington Street to form another cooperative in what was Phase Two. Ironically, what helped at that time was that Margaret Thatcher was in government, looking at how the Militants were carrying on in Liverpool."

Tony decided to go political, which for him meant joining the Labour Party to fight on the inside. He said:

"Ultimately, you have to be voted in to get anywhere. I went to my first local Labour party meeting at the back of St. Anthony's Church on Scotland Road.

"All this shouting was going on because we would not vote for the illegal budget. There were two or three of us, but I realized we needed to get a few more in. I rolled up at the next meeting with 150 people.

"We took control of the Ward and said we were sticking up for national Labour Party policy.

"We saw the coops as the backbone of socialism for us, but we knew it would be a long fight. We continued to negotiate for the Tate & Lyle land.

"They were impressed with us, but it was still a David and Goliath battle."

The site itself had been valued at £250,000. At this point it had been cleared of the buildings, but it remained contaminated

Eldon Street building work in 1904

Tony McGann

industrial land. Later on, surveys revealed that those dangerous contaminates needed to be taken away.

A further complication raised its head when a land search revealed that British Waterways owned the strip of land right down the middle (the canal) and it looked as if this might push the price through the roof.

The Eldonians, on a tight deadline, now had to get English Estates and British Waterways together. Tony McGann had made an unexpected contact in Liverpool in the shape of Colonel McClelland, the Managing Director of Vernons Pools.

Vernon Sangster was the multi millionaire owner of the famous pools company and Tony received a surprise call from him indicating that British Waterways chairman Sir Leslie Young was attending a party at his house on the Isle of Man.

He arranged for Tony to speak to Young and the Eldonian man was not slow in pointing out that the new valuation of the Tate's site was unrealistic. There is no doubt that Colonel McClelland had already briefed the key people and the Eldonians would ultimately get the land for the original £250,000 valuation. They were also given a grant of £2.1m to 'do it up' as Tony modestly puts it.

"It was a massive site with a hell of a lot of contaminates in it," said Tony, who was making trips to London to meet Neil Kinnock. The Labour leader told him: "Stay in the trenches, sonny."

This indicates that there was still a major local political war going on. Indeed, Kinnock would soon make his now famous speech at the Labour Party Conference in October 1985 when he attacked the Militants and their record in the leadership of Liverpool City Council. Kinnock had declared:

"I'll tell you what happens with impossible promises. You start with a series of far-fetched resolutions, and these are then pickled into a rigid dogma, a code, and you go through the years sticking to that, misplaced, outdated, irrelevant to the needs, and you end up in the grotesque chaos of a Labour Council – A LABOUR COUNCIL – hiring taxis to scuttle around the city handing out redundancy notices to its workers. I tell you – and you'll listen – you can't play politics with people's jobs and people's homes and people's services."

Labour MP Eric Heffer walked off the platform and Derek Hatton repeatedly shouted "liar" at Kinnock from the floor.

The previous year, in June 1984, the Secretary of State for the Environment, Patrick Jenkin, had visited Vauxhall Road to see the housing conditions for himself and hear about the Eldonians' plans. This was a great opportunity to convince a key government official that the Eldonians had all the qualities to manage the new development

Tony McGann (right) in the Eldonian Village, speaking to resident Lynne Edwards

once it was completed. Jenkin was escorted up Burlington Street, accompanied by Tony McGann, Mickey Keating, Billy Little and Jack McBane.

The Portland Gardens development was explained to him, and he was informed about the plans to utilize the large Tate's site to build houses for the remaining members of the community.

He then viewed the *'We'll do a better job ourselves'* exhibition at the Eldonian tenements headquarters. Jenkin was impressed that the Eldonians wanted to communicate and work with the government, not just abuse them as political opposites.

At the end of 1984, the funding for the Eldonian Village was approved in principle with a notional figure confirmed in the 1984/85 Housing Corporation budget for both the land reclamation and the building.

It was 1987 before the final costings were approved, but the important thing was that a binding agreement was in place and this was a massive boost for the Eldonians.

The design process would now begin to unfold and so the people could actually begin to see and fully understand the vision for their future homes.

One major issue early on was how the Eldonians would allocate the houses. George Evans explained the highly unusual solution.

He said:

"We had a big plan showing all of the houses

and bungalows. We had local priest Father Dunne on the Bingo Machine to make sure of total fairness. People were each given a number.

"If you wanted to live next door to an old neighbour or a relative, you would both be given the same number. The machine was started and if your number popped up, you came forward to look at the plan and select a house in the category you were entitled to.

"That's how the houses were allocated. Ironically, Tony McGann's was one of the last numbers to come out!"

By 1987, one thing remained unresolved. It emerged that the Eldonians would now require Planning Permission for the Tate's site and that pitched them headlong into a new confrontation with their Militant adversaries on the City Council.

Tony McGann recalls:

"The Press were everywhere when the news originally broke that we'd got the money for the site development. We thought we were out of the claws of the Militants. Of course, we then suddenly realised that we had to go for planning permission! Well, they were waiting for us.

"They refused us on the grounds of 'noxious smells'.

"I've lived here all my life. There were smells, but no one was bothered about it then. But because we wanted to build cooperative houses on there, suddenly the smells went right up your nostrils. Anyhow, we took it to a public enquiry that was held at Liverpool's Central Library in October 1985.

"All the council's barristers were there. The councillors were there, and all we had were the old parishioners.

"Then who walked in wearing his full robes? It was Roman Catholic Archbishop Derek Worlock.

"Anglican Bishop David Sheppard was not at the enquiry, but he too would later stand shoulder to shoulder with Worlock at subsequent Eldonian rallies and at the opening of the site. They were the greatest friends we ever had. The Militants sunk in their boots."

Archbishop Worlock had said:

"If you move these people on against their will, I'm going to stand shoulder to shoulder with them in this street."

The Council retained their position about the Tate's site being contaminated and their barrister held up detailed plans, explaining how the smell would get blown by westerly winds to make it impossible for anybody to live there. Meanwhile, the Eldonians barrister just sat there without saying a word.

Tony explained:

"After about 45 minutes the inspector asked if there were 'any questions?' Our barrister said: 'Before you sit down, just to clarify, you're saying the Westerly winds will blow here?' 'Yes they will', said the council barrister. 'Are you sure?' our man replied. 'I'm positive!' said his opponent.

"Our barrister brought the house down when he said: 'You do know that you've been standing with those plans upside down for the last 45 minutes?'

"There was uproar. I was then asked if I was cross with the Council and if I was leading people astray by asking them to move to a 'poisonous site'. I said: 'Not as angry as you'.

The final decision went to Home Secretary Kenneth Baker in London. The Eldonians won and Tony McGann was asked to go to 10 Downing Street to meet the Prime Minister. Tony was told not to ask her for money.

He sat there while Margaret Thatcher spoke about the importance of small shops. She was proud that her parents had run one in Grantham. She then said:

"Do you know, Mr McGann, Ronald Reagan was sitting in your chair last night!"

Thatcher, of course, was renowned for her special relationship with the American President.

Tony didn't ask for money, but ultimately Liverpool was given another £14m for Phase Two of the Eldonian Village, and Riverside Housing's Athol Village further up Vauxhall Road. Tony McGann was actually the very last person to move out of Burlington Street, something that re-emphasised the determination of the Eldonians to show fairness.

He recalls:

"I was sleeping up there with 200 empty flats."

No doubt hundreds of rats as well, Tony!

Today, the Eldonian project retains its incredible momentum.

Tony says:

"People couldn't wait to get out of here because of the lack of opportunities and jobs. But we stood our ground and now we are inundated with people wanting to come back. We've got a ten year waiting list!"

George Evans added:

"The ironic thing is it's not about the type of houses that we build. Some of the applications we get are from people living in houses far younger than ones we could offer them. But it's the sense, or perception, of safety, and community.

"And it doesn't just manage itself. It takes a lot of hard work to keep on top of it. People think it's the easiest job in the world trying to manage the Eldonian Village, but in fact it's the hardest, because once you're on the top there's only one way you can go.

"We've had so many people wanting to visit us to see how it's done that we've had to restrict it to one a month. Luckily enough, me and Tony get invited to speak all over the world too."

Tony smiled and said:

"I did a talk in the German Reichstag in Berlin, and I've also talked about our project in places like Pittsburg, and New York."

George added:

"He gets to go to the nice places. I end up in the Women's Institute in Aintree – with no disrespect whatsoever to those ladies!

"We've built two care homes on the Eldonian site, so we can keep the elderly people here. We've just built 40 apartments for those over 55, but we're also trying to get private developers in to build too.

"Unlike other coops, we're not just static. What annoys me and Tony when we speak with other coops is that once they've achieved their

The Leeds-Liverpool Canal looking towards the Eldonian Village

aim to build, say, twenty or thirty houses, they stop. It is such a waste – all that education and knowledge wasted."

There also has to be a plan to get the right community mix.

Tony explained:

"In the first phase, we had older people. In the second phase we agreed that 75% of the residents would be young families. If we didn't do that the schools would close. They're the future.

"Now we're involved in some apprenticeships to try and get our young people back to work."

George Evans summed up the aims of the Eldonians.

He said:

"We aim, as the group, to look at housing, health, education, employment, and safety. If we can have an input in all of these things, we will definitely create a far better sustainable community, and a happier, more productive, population."

You can't help but be impressed with the Eldonians, which brings me back to my opening thoughts. So could it all have been different for the adjacent district of Everton where I once lived before the 1960s slum clearance exodus?

Clearly, the Eldonians had to go to war

to fulfill their dreams. Anyone who thought it would be a sprint, soon realized that they would have to run a hundred marathons, but every long stride was worth it.

Tony summed it up this way:

"After 20 years, old women come up to me and say: 'Tony, we still feel as if we are on our holidays.'"

That says it all for me. My grandmother, Emily Rogers, was bulldozed out of one of those steep Everton streets in the Sixties and ended up in a soulless high rise in Croxteth.

She died there and I can guarantee that she never felt as if she was on her holidays.

From her isolated flat several storeys up, she would look down at the cemetery below on Dwerryhouse Lane and say:

"Don't bother with the lift. Just lower me down there."

She always had a twinkle in her eye, a sign of defiance from a woman who had grown up steeped in her local Everton community where people cared and people listened.

Thank god the community leaders around Vauxhall Road cared, listened and acted so that their senior citizens, families, friends and neighbours could remain in their spiritual home.

A fascinating view along the old Everton Terrace, with the new high rise blocks taking shape across the ridge while the old terraced streets look a sorry sight. Heyworth Street School can be seen (top middle) with Copeland Street in its shadow where my father and grandparents lived. Other streets along this run included Stonewall, Hibbert, Abbey, Waterhouse, Druid, Jefferson, Sampson and Kepler

THEY TRIED TO MAKE THE NEW STREETS IN THE SKIES SEEM LIKE PROPER HOUSES BUT IT WAS A DISASTER

It takes just one decision to demolish a community built up over a hundred years – it takes decades to get back to where you were, assuming you can get there at all

AS my research into this book reached its conclusion, I returned to Vauxhall Road and the banks of the Leeds-Liverpool Canal to meet George Evans, Chief Executive of the Eldonians.

I was still hung up on this question about whether or not Everton and Scottie Road could have somehow escaped the devastation wreaked by the bulldozers throughout the 1960s and into the 1970s.

As a former Everton boy and Liverpool Corporation housing employee who later crossed the divide to help pick up the vision offered by the new housing cooperatives, I wanted George to consider whether the 'clearances' were truly unavoidable?

Quite simply, could they have knocked down one street, found temporary alternative accommodation for the residents, built proper new houses on the demolished site and then offered people the option of picking up their lives alongside their old friends and neighbours? Was the disastrous High Rise experiment genuinely the only viable solution of any magnitude for the district of Everton at that time?

Could it have all been so radically different? George can look out of his office window these days and scan the remarkable success story that is the Eldonian Village. I asked him if the wider Everton and Scottie Road housing solution was simply too big for the Sixties and Seventies planners. Were they just overwhelmed by the challenge? And what part did local politics play in the outcome?

Obviously, there is no simple answer to this, but George is probably one of those best placed to have an understanding of both sides of the debate.

He said:

"An important factor was the way social housing was funded in that period. The Council received funding per acre based on the number of people ultimately housed within that space. The more you re-housed on one site, the more grant you received.

"This is why the initial multi storey blocks, like the Braddocks and Netherfield Brow, were built higher to take many more tenants. The smaller 'Italian' blocks like Garabaldi, Mazzini and Cavour came later.

"For the Council, it was how to re-house as many families as possible with the scarce financial resources they had at the time.

"High Rise provided a solution, but the people suffered. The planners tried to compensate by calling these giants 'streets in the skies'.

"The flats even had two floors (maisonettes) to try and maintain the concept of living in a house, even if it was one in the sky. The early ones even had coal fires, but it could never be the same for the residents."

Despite the fact that many people were initially grateful to finally live in a property with an inside toilet, bathroom and hot running water, the High Rise blocks quickly deteriorated into a community nightmare.

George recalls:

"I was born in 1954 and we initially lived with my mother's parents in Conyers Street off Netherfield Road. Then we had our first house in Smith Street which was a maisonette. They were slums when we moved in.

"I cannot remember anything that made it a joy to live there. We had running water, but mainly down the walls! But it was the first place my parents could call home.

"Many people will remember when the stables went on fire behind Smith Street. We were evacuated and watched the fire while standing in our pyjamas."

In 1961, after demolition, George's family took a council house in Fazakerley.

He said:

"It was as if we had moved to the country. It reminded me of when we used to go through the Mersey Tunnel as kids and cheer when we got to the other side because we thought we were in Wales!

"It was probably easier for the youngsters to adapt to a move to a large council estate. My mother still used to come back down to shop in 'Greaty' so old habits die hard. My dad would drink in his old haunts off Netherfield Road. Back in Fazakerley, we could catch field mice instead of chasing rats.

"I went to a nice school, Formosa Drive. In Smith Street, most people were Protestants and we all went to the same school. It was much more mixed in Fazakerley and it broke down many of the old religious problems."

But could people like the Evans family, my own family, and the thousands of others affected by the 'clearances' have benefited from a very different Council vision with a complete understanding of the importance of community?

Could the eventual Eldonian solution have been implemented earlier on a wider scale across the district, or was the Sixties demolition programme and solution an inevitability, based on the knowledge of the day and funding available at the time?

George said:

"The cost of building houses is the same, whether it is on a site of demolished houses or in a new town like Skelmersdale. Sometimes it can be cheaper to build on an old site because much of the infrastructure is already in place.

"But you have to accept that it is a long haul

rather than short term fix. It's about informed choices. When the decision was taken to build those new towns on the outskirts, I suspect the planners didn't take into account the social elements like being part of an established community, and safety. Kirkby has only got its identity in the last seven years.

"It takes just one decision to demolish a whole community that has been built up over a hundred years, but it can take decades to get back to where you were (in terms of little shops, schools, churches, and community togetherness).

"This is assuming you can get there at all. You can plan to get it right and make it worthwhile, but you can't force people into change.

"It's not just about the houses when a community is broken up. You lose employers in the area and the local economy becomes depressed."

George believes that in the era of the 1960s clearances, it was more difficult to make informed choices because the housing cooperatives ultimately used by the Eldonians had not really sprung up.

He said:

"It was a time when regeneration was owned by Liverpool City Council. The only choice you had as a tenant was what colour your front door might be, and even then it was only red or green. When I worked in the Council, some people were even questioning whether we should give people a choice of colour!

"Also, the politicians had their own interests at heart. I remember one saying to me: 'Do you know what George? If we solved all of the housing problems in Liverpool, what would the people come to see me about?'"

What indeed? I'm certainly not going to get on my political high horse and declare that it should have all been so different. It's just that the lessons of the Eldonians highlight that

Looking towards Everton Terrace with St. George's Hill to the right and the so-called 'streets in the skies' all round

it is possible to put people first, and this is something every planner worth his or her salt should fully understand now and moving into the future.

Thankfully, the modern Everton has many outstanding individuals fighting for the current community, striving with every sinew to progress the regeneration initiatives that sit on the table.

People on the ground are seeking to inspire the young people into believing that there is a future worth getting up for in the morning.

Everton Ward Councillor Jane Corbett, who is also the Council's Cabinet Member for Education and Children's Services has lived in Everton for over 30 years now and knows the community well.

She said:

"Most Everton people genuinely care for each other and relationships are strong. The district is like a huge family. Everton is a reflection of how a district should be, about being human in a world increasingly overwhelmed by technology. People meet face to face and talk, rather than communicating through computers and emails.

"This reflects back to the fact that the old district was an open door heartland in which people cared.

"You mention a name and it's like putting a plug into a socket; all the lights come on.

"Friends and neighbours know each other and still look out for each other. They will check if someone needs any shopping done. They will try and ensure that the older residents don't feel isolated.

"There is a lot of poverty in the area. People die younger in Everton. The high levels of chronic stress and anxiety in the area undermine people's health, and when there is a massive gap in incomes, everyone suffers from the fracturing of society, but especially those on the lowest incomes.

"It's frustrating because the kids have so many dreams, and yet they are the ones who are now being made to suffer the effects of the Government cuts.

"There is inequality and injustice, but the community always fights back. There is a real desire to keep our community safe. We never talk about Everton being an 'estate'. We always call it a community.

"We have a saying in West Everton: 'It always takes ten years to make things happen!' And yet the community have managed to get a lot done over the last 30 years.

"The housing has been totally transformed through a number of community initiatives including Langrove Street Housing Co op, the Islington Action Group, Radcliffe Street Action Groups, the 4 Beds residents group, and the St Martin Mews Sheltered Scheme

"Two health centres were saved from closure and a new centre built on Everton Road.

"Everton Park was redesigned to include a nature garden and play areas. More recently, the Friends of Everton Park has been set up, growing and heritage projects started, public art projects are being planned, and the 'Out of the Blue' community-run arts festival in the park goes from strength to strength.

"The Friary School has been saved from closure, becoming a joint Catholic and Anglican Primary School with a new building and renamed Faith Primary.

"Great Homer Street, or 'Greaty', is about to be totally regenerated and will include the rebuilding of Notre Dame Catholic College.

"We also want to make Everton Park a special place for people and we want very green, beautiful and sustainable housing on the edges of the park.

"Since the mid 1980s we've been rebuilding West Everton together. We've still got some way to go but we'll get there. I first came to Everton when I was 17 and stayed, and I have to say I love it. This is where I've learned what true community spirit is, from the people of Everton."

Jane sums up perfectly the spirit and determination of the modern Everton.

Whenever I go back into my old district I feel hugely proud to meet real people with no side to them. I always feel as if I'm going home and I'm proud to be one of them.

There is still a huge interest in the old inner city streets,
highlighted by a packed St. George's Church at one of the
'Lost Tribe of Everton and Scottie Road' street reunions

WALK THE WALK TALK THE TALK

IT HAS been quite a journey for every member of the 'Lost Tribe of Everton & Scottie Road'.

Your memories have inspired me, made me laugh and stirred my emotions. Most of all, they have made me feel very proud.

But before we stride together towards my concluding chapter, I want you to join me on a little detour, a walk into the past across the summit of Mount Everton with my starting point inside the grounds of St. George's Church at the junction of St. Domingo Road and Heyworth Street.

This is linked with an on-going project to introduce a Heritage Trail across the top of Everton Park, linking the famous 1814 'Iron Church' with old Everton Village itself.

This idea has been inspired by a team from within the *Friends of Everton Park*.

I am delighted to be a part of this group that wants to remind visitors to the Park what an historic and treasured green space this is.

It manifests itself most spectacularly around the viewing area, above what was the old Everton Terrace from where you can take in breathtaking views of the city below, the River Mersey, the Wirral peninsula in the middle distance and the mountains of North Wales beyond.

It is crucial that the Park is maintained and utilised for the benefit of the people of Everton and visitors alike who recognise the importance of this spectacular site.

The ambitious and longer term Biennial Art project will hopefully be the main catalyst for change, while the Heritage Trail can be a short term win.

Stroll across the summit of Mount Everton and feel supremely proud of this historic district

Under the greenery of the modern Park lies many of those hundreds of steep streets that were once home to the 'Lost Tribe of Everton' and there is no doubt that the district is still viewed by thousands all over the city as their spiritual home.

The Heritage Trail, if we can make it happen, would have up to 15 information boards, linking the English Civil War with the English Premier League.

Everton, of course, was the place where professional football began in a city renowned worldwide for its two famous football clubs.

It has been a pleasure to be involved in the vision for this trail, working alongside the tireless John Hutchison, chairman of the board of management at the outstanding Shrewsbury House Youth and Community Centre, plus Jimmy Fearns, Adam Byrne, Jo Hayes, Erica Hedley and Tom Corbett.

Sam Perry, Bob Harrington and Laurie Peake have also provided input.

So if you are up for a stroll into Everton history, join me on the pages that follow, beginning in that St. George's churchyard.

Here you should stand and imagine how our ancestors sent messages warning of imminent danger, possibly the arrival of an invading army or navy.

The lighting of the Everton Fire Beacon was the ancient version of sending a text on your mobile phone.

In many respects, it was equally effective because messages could be flashed across the country extremely quickly via these hilltop sites.

Read on to find out more . . .

BEACON LANE

The Everton Fire Beacon (1230-1803)

The Everton Beacon was the tallest building in ancient Everton, commanding the highest point on the ridge. It was built by Ranulf – the Earl of Chester, the first baron of Liverpool – on the site of the present St. George's Church during the reign of King Henry III (1207-1272). When lit, the Beacon could be seen for miles around. Fire Beacons occupied high ground right across the country to warn of imminent danger. Indeed, the Everton Beacon and others like it were lit when the Spanish Armada was sighted in the English Channel during the reign of Queen Elizabeth 1st. For centuries, Everton's famous landmark was a feature of both the local geography and community life. Hundreds of people would gather below it to picnic and relax in what is now Everton Park. Towards the end of the 18th century, the tower was becoming unsafe and it was severely damaged on a stormy night in 1803.

Eleven years later the site had been cleared to make way for the new St. George's Church, but the path approaching it from the north side would ultimately become Beacon Lane to mark an historic Everton landmark.

1

NORTHUMBERLAND TERRACE

St. George's 'Iron Church'

The Fire Beacon site would make way for one of Everton's most famous landmarks. St. George's Church was the vision of merchant James Atherton (1770-1838) who bought a sizeable piece of land across the top of Everton Ridge. Atherton comissioned a string of luxurious hilltop mansions, each with spectacular views of the River Mersey and Wirral beyond. He recognised the need for a church to serve the needs of the growing local merchant population and raised £11,500 by public subscription. The church was completed in 1814 on the old Beacon site, directly opposite Atherton's own mansion. The innovative ideas of church architect Thomas Rickman (1776-1841) included a cast iron frame clad with local sandstone. The revolutionary use of iron would ultimately lead to the erection of much higher structures, like Liverpool's classic Liver Building, and many of the early skyscrapers across the Atlantic in places like New York. From his garden, Atherton could see a 'Black Rock' across the river to the North West and this would take him 'over the water' to plan the famous Mersey seaside resort of New Brighton. His love of Everton never waned. On his death, Atherton was brought back to St. George's and buried in the churchyard.

2

HEYWORTH STREET

Victoria Cross heroes in the heart of Everton

From St. George's Church, you should now walk into Everton Park and take the top path to a point beyond the former Thistle Pub, now May Duncan's. Here stood the old Heyworth Street School which is just one of the sites in Everton with links to the Victoria Cross, the highest and most prized military decoration any member of our armed forces can be awarded for courage in the face of the enemy. Two words on the Victoria Cross say everything about those who have earned this ultimate accolade: FOR VALOUR. The VC takes precedence over all other orders, decorations and medals and may be awarded to a person of any rank in any service and to civilians under military command.

Introduced on 29 January 1856 by Queen Victoria to honour acts of valour during the Crimean War, the medal – at the time of writing - has been awarded 1,356 times to 1,353 individual recipients. Only 13 medals, nine to members of the British Army, and four to the Australian Army, have been awarded since the Second World War, demonstrating that this is a medal that

is truly one of the most treasured of war accolades anywhere in the world.

Sixteen VC's have been awarded to Liverpool heroes, a record that demonstrates the wider courage, fortitude and character of the men of our city who have never been found wanting when their country has needed them, something that is still evident today in places like Afghanistan and previously in Iraq, the Falklands, and other modern theatres of war.

3

One thing that fills me with pride is that four of those 16 Victoria Crosses were won by men, not all born in Everton, but with massive links to the very heart of the area where I lived as a kid (David Jones; Paul Aloysius Kenna, Gabriel George Coury; Albert White).

I always knew about Sgt. David Jones VC. Like my father Harry Rogers, he went to Heyworth Street School. My dad always proudly told me the story of the soldier from the King's Liverpool Regiment whose military courage brought reflected glory on every inner city youngster who attended Heyworth Street and looked up at the famous brass plaque on the school wall that declared:

> To the memory of
> **Serg. David Jones VC**
> **The King's (Liverpool Regiment)**
> *An old pupil of this school, who was awarded the Victoria Cross during the Great War for his inspiring courage and cheering example. When his officers, having all fallen, he took command, captured an advanced position on the Somme front, and in spite of the fiercest counter attacks, held it for nearly three days, until relieved. He was killed in action three weeks later on October 7th 1916.*
> **"Qui ante diem, perit**
> **Sed miles, sed pro patria"**

I believe this translates to:
"They died before their time
But as soldiers, and for their country"

An old Liverpool Echo cutting featuring a 1950s column written by the famous George Harrison (the journalist, not the

'FOR VALOUR IN THE

▶ Beatle) reminded us of Jones' courage. He featured a citation in the London Gazette a fortnight after Jones was killed. It quoted one of the men who served with him:

"We walked right into hell through the back door and suffered terribly (occupying the position for two days and two nights without food or water). We were like sheep without a shepherd until chirpy, cheerful Davy Jones took charge. It was mainly because of him that we got through."

I found myself reading a fantastic publication entitled: *Liverpool Heroes (Book 1), the stories of 16 Liverpool holders of the Victoria Cross,* edited and researched by Ann Clayton, with further research by Sid Lindsay and Bill Sergeant. I had met Bill at the hugely popular Radio Merseyside Big History Day at St. George's Hall and it was only when I got home and engrossed myself in 'Liverpool Heroes' that I realised that he also came from Everton. He had attended Everton Methodist Church as a youngster while I attended St. George's.

In the book foreword, Bill used a biblical quotation from John 15.13: *'Greater love hath no man than this; that a man lay down*

his life for his friends'.

It has been used on the headstones of many soldiers, notably one of Liverpool's most respected war heroes Noel Chavasse VC and Bar (in other words a double Victoria Cross recipient).

The words sum up perfectly that moment of selfless courage when someone steps right into the firing line with no regard to their own safety.

If you get a chance to read Liverpool Heroes, please do, not least because all proceeds from the sale of the book have been going to the Noel Chavasse VC Memorial Association whose objective is to maintain the memorial that has been erected to our city's greatest heroes, while promoting awareness within local schools and communities.

I instinctively flicked through to the David Jones chapter, but very quickly I grasped the remarkable Everton link between Jones, Paul Aloysius Kenna VC DSO, Gabriel George Coury VC, and Albert White VC.

In 1901, the Jones' family were living at 25 Elmore Street, Everton. As explained, the young David Jones attended Heyworth Street School on the top of Everton's famous ridge. On 27 May, 1915, he married Elizabeth Dorothea Doyle, and they went to live at 87 Heyworth Street. Jones won his VC on the night of 4/5 September 1916.

Paul Aloysius Kenna was born half a mile

3

FACE OF THE ENEMY'

down the hill from Heyworth Street, at Oakfield House, 22 Richmond Terrace, on 16 August 1862.

At the age of seven, Paul attended St. Francis Xavier's School in Salisbury Street. He was later commissioned as a Lieutenant in a Militia Battalion of the Durham Light Infantry.

Kenna would eventually join the 21st Lancers, stationed in India, and he became the leading gentleman rider in India. He found himself in Ireland in 1895 where he rescued a man from the River Liffey in Dublin, receiving the Royal Humane Society's 'Vellum Testimonial'. In 1895 he was promoted to Captain, and the following year went with the Lancers to Egypt.

He found himself part of an Anglo-Egyptian Expeditionary Force marching on Khartoum where the legendary British Governor of the Sudan, General Charles Gordon, had been murdered.

On 2 September, 1895, the 21st Lancers were ordered to advance between a prominent hill and the River Nile to harass the enemy's flank, believing they were facing just a few hundred Dervishes. The Lancers advanced at a gallop and

David Jones VC

as they closed on the enemy, raced forward when ordered to "Charge!" Suddenly 3,000 white robed Dervishes appeared on the ridges on their flank and the Lancers were trapped and under severe enemy gunfire.

There was no option but to wheel round and cut their way back through the massed enemy ranks.

The tribesmen targeted the horses, leaving the unseated soldiers to fight for their lives on foot. Kenna, second in command to Major Fowle in one of four squadrons, used his superb horsemanship to get through. The Lancers dismounted and pinpointed withering fire on the Dervishes who, despite their numbers, retreated with 2,000 repelled by 300 Lancers.

It was highlighted that Kenna and B Squadron went into the most densely packed area of the enemy line, highlighted by the fact his squadron won all three VC's awarded that day.

At one point in the mayhem, Kenna stopped his horse and used his revolver to enable the dismounted Major W.G. Crole-Wyndham to climb up behind him. The unsettled horse then threw both Lancers after 50 yards. Kenna retrieved the horse while Crole-Wyndham escaped on foot and both rejoined the line.

The 'Liverpool Heroes' book reveals

JONES, KENNA, COURY,

▶ that in December 1906 Kenna was appointed aide de camp to King Edward VII. Sadly, there would be no happy ending for this brave former SFX boy. He became Brigadier General of the Midlands Mounted Division, but was shot by a Turkish sniper's bullet on 29 August 1915 and died the next day.

Gabriel George Coury VC was born in Sefton Park, but is another SFX boy, attending the Salisbury Street School between 1901 and May 1907. At the start of the First World War, he enlisted as a Private in the King's (Liverpool) Regiment.

After training, his leadership qualities were recognised when he was made a 2nd Lieutenant in the South Lancashire Regiment. He went to France in 1915 with his regiment designated a Pioneer battalion and the following year found himself in the middle of the disastrous Battle of the Somme, a war of attrition in the trenches.

On 5 August Coury was in a trench under heavy bombardment when explosives suddenly ignited. There was panic amongst the troops who believed the Germans were making a bomb attack. As many tried to leave the trenches, Coury picked up a rifle and bayonet and took charge to get the men back in position.

This highlighted his leadership qualities. His moment of true 'Valour' leading to his Victoria Cross was reported by the London Gazette:

During an advance he was in command of two platoons ordered to dig a communication trench from the old firing line to the positions won. By his fine example and utter contempt for danger, he kept up the spirits of his men and completed his task under heavy fire. Later, after the Battalion with whom he was working suffered heavy casualties and the Commanding Officer had been wounded, he went out in front of the advancing position, and in full daylight, in full view of the enemy, he found the Commanding Officer and brought him back to safety over ground swept with machine gun fire. He not only completed his original task and then saved the Commanding Officer, but he also succeeded in rallying the attacking troops when they were shaken, and leading them forward.

Coury was only 20 years of age and was only eight years out of SFX School. The boy had become a very brave man and an eye witness declared to the Liverpool Daily Post that he was *"the bravest officer I ever served under."*

3

WHITE – OUR VC HEROES

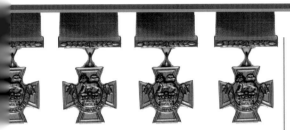

The fourth Victoria Cross with an Everton link was won by Albert White. He was born in Kirkdale, at 54 Lamb Street, but his father educated him at Everton Terrace School in the heart of what is now Everton Park. On 23 October 1915 he enlisted with the Royal Army Medical Corps, and was then transferred to the 2nd Battalion of the South Wales Borderers.

In 1916, Albert found himself in France with his Battalion, now part of the 87th Brigade in the 29th Division. Like Coury and Jones, he was at the deadly Battle of the Somme. He was promoted to Sergeant and his Battalion was told to attack the strongly defended German position at Beaumont Hamel where they had constructed strongly fortified dugouts.

White and his men faced devastating machine gun fire and the battalion lost 11 officers with 235 men killed or missing and a further four officers and 149 men wounded. This was from a total of 21 officers and 578 men.

'Liverpool Heroes' tells us that the 2nd Battalion had to be reformed and saw fresh action in 1917 at Monchy-le-Preux where Albert White earned his VC at the Battle of Arras. Despite being under heavy enemy fire, White and his men dashed towards the enemy position.

During the 'rush', a concealed German machine gunner opened fire, threatening the advance.

Sergeant White raced ahead of his men to capture the gun. He flew at the enemy, shooting three and bayoneting a fourth, but was riddled with bullets as he got within yards of the gun, and was killed.

Doesn't it make you feel fiercely proud to come from the city of Liverpool?

If, like me, you are from Everton, doesn't it feel you with extra pride when you consider the strong links of these particular four heroes with our famous district?

We salute David Jones VC; Paul Aloysius Kenna VC DSO; Gabriel George Coury VC; Albert White VC.

■ I thank the authors of *'Liverpool Heroes: The stories of 16 Liverpool holders of the VC'* for their tremendous research and heartfelt input into a book that I would commend you all to read.

HEYWORTH STREET

Prince Rupert's Old Camp Field (1644)

You don't have to move very far from your position on the old Heyworth Street School site to get a feel for one of the most remarkable episodes in the history of Everton. Indeed, you are now standing in the middle of a giant English Civil War Royalist army headquarters that spread out across the ridge at this point. The image above shows the modern site. Obviously, Heyworth Street itself was nothing more than a path in the 1600s. It was Prince Rupert of the Rhine who brought a 10,000 strong Royalist force to Everton in May 1644. Liverpool's population was just over 2,000 at the time. The Castle and Town Hall in the town below had been taken by the Royalists in 1642. The Parliamentarians reclaimed Liverpool the following year and Everton would now become the springboard for a fresh Royalist attack in the name of the King Charles 1. The Royalist army – with horses, munitions and supplies – set up camp across the ridge at this point with uninterrupted views of the town below. The heart of the camp is marked these days by the excellent Campfield Pub. Rupert claimed Liverpool was *'Nought but a crow's nest that a parcel of boys could take.'* However, he was surprised by the resistance he met, even though all the women and children had been evacuated to The Wirral. In fact, Rupert lost 1,500 men before finally breaching the defences and slaughtering around 360 of the defenders. The Royalists plundered the town's gold bullion. Legend has it that Rupert buried it in a tunnel near to his Everton Village headquarters, meaning to claim it at a later date. However, the Parliamentarians recaptured the town before the year was out. The gold horde was never found despite the efforts of many treasure hunters and could still lie below the steep slopes of Everton.

EVERTON TERRACE

The greatest view in Liverpool

You now take the park path to the viewing area and car park a few hundred yards away with its commanding views across the city and the river beyond. This gives you a complete understanding as to why Prince Rupert chose this spot to plan his deadly attack on Liverpool.

Everton ridge may only be 245 feet above sea level, but the panorama from left to right (south to north) is a sight to behold. The horizon is dominated by the Snowdonia mountain range featuring the highest mountain in Wales (Snowdon 1,055 metres). The Wirral Peninsula bridges the middle distance from the Mersey to the unseen River Dee. This is a powerful watery border between England and North Wales. On the far side of the Mersey you can see the large grey box-like structure that is the globally famous Cammell Laird shipyard, built in 1828. This stands in Birkenhead which, with Seacombe to its right, is part of the triangular route of the renowned Mersey Ferries. The Mersey has always been at the heart of Liverpool's development. The town emerged from a small and muddy pool and creek, as a new town and borough, granted a charter as such by King John in 1207. This initially tiny community would go on to become the second city of the British Empire as the 20th century dawned. To your left, the distinctive Anglican and Metropolitan Roman Catholic Cathedrals rise up. The world famous Liver Building and the Radio City Beacon Tower can also be seen. Everton Terrace, with its many large Victorian residences, ran below here into the heart of the old Everton Village.

5

ST. GEORGE'S HILL

'Clearances' create the 'Lost Tribe of Everton'

As you take in the view from Everton ridge, stand still and imagine what lies unseen beneath the modern Everton Park. You are in the heart of what was once a remarkable concrete jungle of back to back terraced houses, standing in hundreds of steep streets sweeping down from this ridge.

This was a sight to behold prior to the 1960s when the 'clearances' changed the face of Everton forever. Over 125,000 residents were forced to leave this historic district for new towns and estates on the outer limits of the city. The clearances are now part of Everton folklore, captured in a song written by Harry and Gordon Dixon entitled Back Buchanan Street.

'We'll miss the Mary Ellens and me Dad'll miss the docks.
And me Gran'll miss the wash house where she washed me Grandad's socks
Don't wanna go to Kirkby, or Skelmersdale or Speke
Don't want to go from all we know in Back Buchanan Street'

Back Buchanan Street did not exist, but could have been any street in Everton, like St. George's Hill, which climbed up from Netherfield Road between Everton Terrace and Northumberland Terrace. In these streets, open-door heartland community living made people fiercely proud of their close friends and neighbours.

This heritage trail point would be an opportunity to remember everyone you loved and who might have never known anything but these concrete streets.

6

NETHERFIELD ROAD

The so-called 'Streets in the skies'

As the 1960s 'clearance' programme swept aside the old terraced streets of Everton, this ridge and the land below it became the focal point for a social experiment in High Rise living that would once again dramatically change the face of this famous district. In the early 1800s, this hill had been a farming area and a green and pleasant oasis for the rich merchants who built their large mansions and villas here. A working class army, swollen by many immigrants fleeing the devastating Irish Potato famine of the 1840s, then swept up the hill to claim 'Mount Everton' for their own. The 1960s 'clearances' brought this phase in Everton's social history to a dramatic close. The terraced streets were replaced by 17 High Rise monoliths that stood like upturned dominoes above and below Netherfield Road that runs right and left just 50 yards below the main viewing area. Netherfield Road North & South was also famous for the Orange Lodge bands that would march along its full length, notably on 12 July, when Everton bristled with fervour, noise and passion. The district changed dramatically following the development of the High-Rise giants, described by the architects who didn't have to live there as 'streets in the skies'.

Among those still standing (some with new names) are Crete, Candia, Brynford and Milburn. Others that became famous in their own way included: Corinth, Seacome, Ellis, Edinburgh, The Braddocks, Mazzini, Cavour, Garibaldi, John F. Kennedy Heights, St. George's Heights, and Haigh, Crosbie and Canterbury (later dubbed the 'Piggeries'). High Rise Heaven deteriorated over 20 years into High Rise Hell. Everton was part of a social experiment that has resonance to this day.

7

EVERTON VILLAGE

Using the famous Everton Lock-Up as a marker, the Heritage Trail walk will now take you from the spectacular viewing area down into the heart of the ancient village of Everton, first recorded in the Domesday Book of 1086. The village was known as 'Evreton' in 1094; as 'Euerton' in 1201; and as 'Everton' since the end of the 13th century.

Whether the name Everton derives from the Celtic-Roman for 'wild boar' or is simply a shortening of Higher Town, the village has a fascinating history.

Standing above the Lock-Up on Brow Side, looking up the hill, you can now imagine what Everton Village was like from the Herdman picture above, with sheep being driven up Village Street. The image, from the 1800s, captures the sleepy feel of the village.

The population of Everton had remained static for centuries, a settled and relatively isolated village.

Even in 1801, the population was recorded as being only 499, and the Village grew up around an area that had previously been known as 'Sandstone Hill'.

However, during the English Civil War, in the mid 17th century (1642-51), the tranquillity and isolation of the village came to an abrupt end, and Everton suddenly took on a strategic importance.

8

9   BROW SIDE

Prince Rupert's Cottage

The cottage stood across a track, immediately to the right of the Lock-Up as you look down the hill, it was named after Prince Rupert of the Rhine (1619-1682), the nephew of King Charles I (1600-1649). The Prince stood against the Parliamentary forces and organised the siege of Liverpool. He established his Royalist headquarters here on Brow Side. After the Civil War ended, Prince Rupert's Cottage became an ordinary home once more and, for many years, it was occupied as a family property before being demolished in 1845.

The Everton Toffee Shop

The Everton Toffee Shop

Around 1690, another larger cottage was built next to Prince Rupert's old cottage and it was here that Molly Bushel (1746-1818) began to make the boiled sweets she called Everton Toffee. This toffee was much prized, not just by locals, but also by the wealthier classes.

In 1783, Molly converted her house into a shop and began to expand her range of confectionery. Later, Everton Toffee, which continued to be made by Molly's descendants, became a great favourite with Queen Victoria, who had batches of it regularly shipped to Windsor Castle. The recipe had been given to Molly by its inventor, Doctor James Gerrard, a local physician and Town Council member. The Everton Toffee Shop was demolished in 1844. Everton Toffee is still produced although not to the original recipe.

Everton Football Club's 'Toffee Lady' mascot still throws sweets to the crowd at every home game.

View of Everton from Rupert Lane, showing
Brow Side, circa 1865 – a watercolour by J. Charter.
See overleaf to find out about the Everton Lock-Up
featured in this remarkable image

EVERTON'S ANCIENT

The Everton Lock-Up

As Everton began to expand, the centre of life in the village was around the village green and Molly Bushel's Toffee Shop, and there was a significant rise in the numbers of visitors to the village. These people came to take the air, to buy the famous toffee, and to see Prince Rupert's old Cottage. Eventually, there were so many day-trippers that, in 1787, it was considered necessary to build a local lock-up 'to house drunks and unruly revellers overnight'.

This became a well-known landmark, sometimes called The Stone Jug, but also called 'Prince Rupert's Castle' by locals although it was erected long after the Prince had gone. It is one of only two surviving village gaols in Liverpool, the other being located in the middle of Wavertree Village to the south of the City. The Tower is the only physical reference to old Everton Village.

You should now walk up Village Street itself – these days devoid of any buildings.

VILLAGE STREET

Football fever started at the Queen's Head Hotel

You will need to use your imagination here, visualising the cottages and houses from the Herdman picture on page 208. The village's main pub, the Queen's Head Hotel, was the scene of an historic meeting in 1879 that led to St. Domingo's Church Football team changing its name to Everton Football Club.

This heralded the start of the city of Liverpool's remarkable football heritage. Everton FC became founder members of the Football League in 1888. Ironically, the club never played in Everton, its original pitch being in Stanley Park, while its main early headquarters was the current home of Liverpool FC in Anfield.

Everton FC built its present Goodison Park Stadium in Walton in 1892, a move that inspired the formation of Liverpool FC to signal one of the greatest rivalries in world football.

However, Everton's roots remain firmly in heartland Everton where it took its name, and from where the original St. Domingo's FC drew many of its early players. The Everton Lock-Up is featured on Everton FC's famous crest, confirming its powerful links with this site. Near to the Queen's Head Hotel, in the middle of Village Street, stood the Village Cross. The market cross stood upon a flight of stone steps until 1820, when it was stolen in a controversial fashion. Historical accounts tell us that the cross had been pronounced a nuisance to traffic, but village residents refused to let the authorities remove it. After one dark and stormy winter's night, the people of Everton awoke to discover that the cross had gone. Who? When? How? Whispers gathered strength and the news spread that the Devil had run off with the Village Cross. There may be more truth to the reports of two men, seen with a wheelbarrow, crowbar, pickaxe and spade on that stormy night – but we shall never know.

The Everton Village Cross in Village Street in 1830 (by W. Herdman)

Aerial views of Everton taken from the roof of St George's Church tower in January, 1949. Above, you can see the John Bagot Hospital in the foreground with the River Mersey in the distance.
Top right, you can see the roof of the Popular Cinema on Netherfield Road North and get a real feel for the back to back terraced streets sweeping down the hill.
Right, is a view towards Anfield with the famous Everton Library immediately below, vibrant and fully operational at that time.
Below right, further down St. Domingo Road, with a great view of the Sir Thomas White tenement blocks

Northumberland Terrace from the St. George's Church tower in 1949, with the Anglican Cathedral clearly visible in the distance

THE JOURNEY HOME
IS COMPLETE

Why we will never forget the famous terraced streets that made us what we are today

I HOPE you enjoyed the previous chapter and your short, but inspiring walk across the pages of Everton's remarkable history.

The 'Lost Tribe of Everton & Scottie Road' has been an all-consuming project over the past three years and I suddenly find myself with hugely mixed emotions.

I started this follow-up book with a short piece of verse under the header: 'Lost Tribe back on sacred ground.'

The first line of a heartfelt poem said it all: 'The journey home is now complete . . . '

But I feel uncomfortable with the word *'complete'*.

It seems as if I'm saying goodbye to my old district for a second time and I feel as if it's all so final, just like it did in 1962 when a removal van pulled up outside 8 Melbourne Street, Everton, Liverpool 5, to take my family to a new life in Norris Green.

That was 50 years ago, but that day is imprinted on my memory. My parents, May and Harry Rogers, were strangely upbeat and excited. After all, we were moving from our concrete jungle to a tree-lined street and a council house with a bathroom, inside toilet, hot running water and neat gardens back and front. I was 14 at the time.

I can't remember if my mum and dad shed a tear. After all, we were leaving the house where my grandparents, Adam and Ethel Wareing, raised seven children – Joe, George, John, Adam (Alan) Jnr., Bobby, May and Ada.

The two-bedroomed terraced property with an attic, a parlour, a kitchen (living room), back kitchen, and tiny backyard had been home to the Wareings and the Rogers for a quarter of a century.

That's an awful lot of memories to drive away from. I remember exactly what I did in the minutes before we slammed the door shut for the very last time.

I went into the now empty front parlour and sat on the floor in front of the bay window with the light streaming in from the street outside. It had never been a room that we used very often, but tell me about a parlour that was.

I shut my eyes and remembered those days in the early 1950s when, as a small boy, I would go in there on a dark winter's evening with my mother as she dressed the Christmas tree. Later, I would get on the floor and crawl right under that tree, cloaked in total darkness except for the magical glow of the colourful tree lights as they flickered on and off above my head.

My mother always put exactly the same decorations on the tree. These included little coloured boxes that looked as if they had intriguing gifts inside them, but which were just for decorative effect. Those flashing lights with their large pear shaped bulbs hung from a thick black wire, creating a warm glow for the little pink fairy that always took pride of place on top of the tree.

The shout of the removal man reminded me that it was actually a summer's day in June, not a dark yet warming Christmas Eve.

With time running out, I picked myself up and quickly climbed the dark, steep stairs off the hall to the first floor landing, with one door to the right (my parents' old front bedroom) and one door to the left, my own bedroom looking down onto the yard below with the back entry and the towering back wall of the old Victoria Settlement community centre beyond.

My small room, the epicentre of my world for so long, looked stark and lonely. It was now devoid of the cast iron bed, the nightly retreat from where, in younger days, I would stare up at my Dan Dare wallpaper and imagine star wars encounters, battling against our sworn enemy, the Mekon. Of course, my imaginary 'Outer Space' adventures would also transport me into Flash Gordon's silver rocket ship en route to another intergalactic battle with the dreaded Ming the Merciless. How did I ever get to sleep?

This room had darker memories. My granddad Adam Wareing had died in there in 1953, just a few short months after taking me down to Westminster Road to see the illuminated Coronation tram. He was just 61. I loved my granddad, and now we were leaving his memories behind as well.

I continued my final tour of the house, skipping along the short landing and up the winding staircase to the rooftop attic.

I'm sure it had been used as a vital bedroom during the early 1940s to accommodate the four Wareing boys who would soon be going to war, but I remember it as a dusty, yet exciting play room, devoid of carpet or even oil cloth, just bare floor boards. In one corner, stood what I now realise must have once been the household treasures, the pride and joy of my grandparents or possibly even their parents, ornate vases like giants versions of the FA Cup, covered with glass domes. I also remember an ornate clock with what looked like a black ivory case.

These would now be left behind by my parents, having been assessed as old fashioned junk by a couple moving to their

Great Homer Street pictured in 1948

new council house on a suburb estate. If only I had those vases now, and that has got absolutely nothing whatsoever to do with monetary value. What a wonderful, tangible memory they would be of the grandfather I idolised and the grandmother I never saw.

Ethel Wareing (nee Bradley) died of a stroke just before I was born.

The only things I retain that belonged to my grandad are an old and heavy cast iron frying pan that used to constantly be on the go on the black range in the kitchen, and a battered old piano stool that could bear witness to a thousand post war sing-songs when the lads came home. My Aunty Ada was a proficient piano player, and my Uncle John, who looked quite Italian to me, was renowned for his outstanding singing voice.

I'm sure there were countless opportunists who quickly broke into those empty Victorian terraced properties as soon as the removal wagons pulled away. How many others left family 'treasures' behind, not wanting to take any 'clutter' to their new world? Probably thousands!

My hope has been that those ornate vases might eventually have found their way into a smart antique shop and that they now have pride of place in a really nice house somewhere, rather than having been smashed to pieces by rampaging kids or destroyed by the wrecking crews who brought in the slum clearance bulldozers. Who knows?

I now raced downstairs for one last look at our kitchen living space with its large open fireplace. How many happy memories had unfolded in this room in front of that roaring fire? How many Christmas mornings had I led my younger sister June down the stairs, launched open the door, and shouted: 'He's been!'

The house was 80 years old. It had been a living, breathing home for close on 30,000 days and nights.

It had survived the 1941 May Blitz, although part of the terrace opposite had been blasted, leaving a wide, deep debris area linking Melbourne Street and Adelaide Street. Similarly, the large houses at the bottom of the street on Netherfield Road had also been obliterated by a devastating parachute mine.

People had been killed in that street. Many more people had been born there, including my sister June (while I was born in Walton

Hospital). We were now being ushered out of our childhood home, our family home, my grandparents' home. I would never play football in that steep street again (after over 3,650 games).

I have explained in some details my final minutes in a place that I clearly felt a spiritual attachment to, even as a young teenage boy of just 14. What I can't remember are any tears in the street outside; any friends and neighbours hugging each other and saying their last goodbyes; any souvenir photographs; any final emotions whatsoever.

It was all over. The king is dead, long live the king! Except Norris Green never shaped up as a kingdom for me. I never felt as if I truly belonged there. I was an Everton boy. I am an Everton boy. And so in July 2010 I committed my memories to the pages of my first 'Lost Tribe of Everton & Scottie Road' book, hoping that they would in turn revive some of your memories.

The response has been stunning. I have been reunited with friends I had not seen for half a century. I have made hundreds of new friends from the old streets. I have taken my project to a much more personal level by organising the 'Lost Tribe of Everton' street reunions, using St. George's Church as a very special base. These annual get-togethers are now part of a vibrant summer Everton events calendar. I have even organised three reunions linked with my famous old primary school, Major Lester, which sadly is facing its own demolition D-Day this year.

At the outset of this project, I set out to provide a fully inter-active 'street website' – www.losttribeofeverton.com – a platform for old friends and neighbours to reconnect from anywhere in the world.

Perhaps the most important part of this website is the street section where you can look up your former Everton address (90% of them presently feature on the site, effectively everything within the triangle formed by Everton Valley, Kirkdale Road, Scotland Road, Byrom Street, Islington, Brunswick Road,

Everton Road, Heyworth Street, and St. Domingo Road back to the Valley, with some extra streets on the periphery).

This information relates to the Electoral Roll from 1960 when the slum clearance programme began to unfold. This searchable section enables you to do nothing more complicated than leave a heartfelt tribute to your parents and grandparents.

Some people have contacted me to say they have been unable to find their streets on the site. The reality is that it was such a massive personal commitment. We managed to key in over 80,000 family entries which took several months of relentless inputting.

I set a Phase 1 challenge and I hope that the other names and addresses will ultimately follow in Phase 2.

To compensate for any streets still to be input, a Memory Tab enables you to leave a tribute, seek out information from fellow 'Lost Tribe' members, or potentially find an old neighbour. Since its launch, thousands of new memories/pieces of information have been submitted and this database grows daily. Of course, it is completely free to use and is clearly a facility that an army of people have taken advantage of.

Since the launch of the first 'Lost Tribe of Everton & Scottie Road' book, an Everton & District History Society has been formed that meets regularly, and if you have a wider interest in the district's history, I would commend you to join.

There is a tremendous amount going on in Everton, like the annual 'Out of the Blue' summer music festival in the park, and the spectacular 'Kite Festival' around the same time.

The Everton Youth Orchestra, operating out of the Faith Primary School, grows in stature and is a truly inspirational way of giving local youngsters a joyful focus on life. Hope University continues to develop and the 'Friends of Everton Park' and 'Friends of St. Francis Xavier' are vibrant and imaginative community groups.

Everton is fighting back and that fills me with hope and optimism that my old district, almost battered into submission in the Sixties and Seventies, is rising like a phoenix from the flames of demolition.

So is the journey home complete as I alluded to in the poem at the start of this book, and in the opening words to this final chapter?

I prefer to look on it as the first step in a long journey. Everyone with a love of Everton and Scottie Road simply cannot afford to relax for a single moment as the district moves into a new phase of development. There is an exciting regeneration plan for 'Greaty' — that legendary old shopping mile — that every single one of us must support to a successful conclusion.

There is an ambitious redevelopment plan for the wider Everton Park that includes the Biennial Art Project.

I would love to see the old Everton Library at the junction of St. Domingo Road and Heyworth Street brought back from the brink of demolition. A team has been working on a funding bid for several months.

Of course, the library would have to recover its old stock of Noddy books, plus those must-have Biggles, and Famous Five favourites, the ultimate prize for every kid scouring its children's section in the early 1950s!

Seriously, this building is a design gem and a key district landmark and it must not be allowed to crumble into oblivion like so much that went before. I believe it could provide a major community focus as well as becoming Centre of Excellence for local family history research in Liverpool and I would certainly offer the full support of the 'Lost Tribe of Everton & Scottie Road' history project as a key strand of that.

I will continue to reach out to those who revel in their old street memories through my regular Saturday column in the Liverpool Echo newspaper and so I will be communicating with many of you down that channel.

If you read my first 'Lost Tribe' book and you have also revelled in this follow-up based on 'The People's Memories' — I thank you from the bottom of my heart for joining me on what began as a very personal journey, but which has become an inspirational march of the wider 'Lost Tribe' through those magical old terraced streets.

We have each held our mother's outstretched hand again and felt safe, and listened to our grandmas talking absolute sense, using some classic words and phrases. Comedian Tom O'Connor's old favourite was: *"If you fall down and break yer leg, don't come running to me!"*

We have trailed in the wake of our energetic mums on one last imaginary shopping expedition along 'Greaty' and popped across the road to the corner shop on an urgent message: *"Me mother said slice the ham thin, and give us a bag of broken biscuits and half a dozen cracked eggs, and stick it on the bill . . ."*

We have gone out to play in the street and remembered all the rules of kick-the-can, hide and seek, rounders, hopscotch, the inevitable street footy and cricket, and 20 more seasonal pastimes that seemed to make the world go round . . .

We've used the 'Dip' methodology to pick sides for our street games or to sort out a deadlock: *"Dip dip dip, my blue ship, sailing on the water, like a cup and saucer, O-U-T spells out."* And if you were OUT, the quick response to turn that round was: *"With a jolly good slap across you face, just like THAT!"*

And I've just remembered that magical word used when a 'chasing' game was in full flow and you didn't want to be caught or ticked . . . ***BARLEY!***

What a fantastic concept. I've decided to use it the next time I'm asked to wash the dishes at home, or undertake any other household chore that might require me getting up out of the armchair. **BARLEY!** And what a great get-out in the office. "Can you hand in that budget spread sheet by lunchtime?" **BARLEY!** There's no arguing with that.

Is this all making any sense to you? If it is, I assume you probably lived in a street around our way, a place where . . .

The girls skipped in twos, threes and even fours in a thick rotating rope, long enough to round up a herd of cattle and manned at either end by a couple of energetic grown-ups: *It should have developed into an Olympic sport.*

Sat in front of a roaring open fire with a long fork making toast: *Why did it taste so much better like that?*

Spent years learning backslang, only to find out that it doesn't count as a foreign language in your GCE 'O'levels. (*Owyay, upidstay is that?*)

We grew up to understand that *"children should be seen and not heard"* and that men should instinctively open doors for women and stand up for them on crowded buses, without somehow feeling as if you have breached someone's human right to open their own doors or stand up or fall down on a bus if they want to!

We have sat down at the kitchen table and had our tea together as a family. *"You can get down when everybody else has finished and when you've eaten a triple portion of boiled cabbage. It's for your own good!"*

We've walked through an open front door without knocking and marched down a neighbour's lobby into the kitchen: *"Me mam said can we borrow a cup of sugar? Oh, sorry Mrs. Sawyer. I didn't know you were in the tin bath!"*

We have had the cane in school without complaining and for some bizarre reason assumed that this is what happened when you caused a riot in class, rather than bringing a court case for brutality and infringement of human rights: I'm not suggesting for one minute that a low key regime of corporal punishment should be brought back, except for causing a riot in class, of course.

You know, I nearly said: *We stood up in the cinema when the national anthem was played.* But that really would be taking us all back to those decades after the Second World War when everyone took a huge deep breath and genuinely thought: *"My god, that was a close call. Never mind backslang as a second language. How's your German?"*

I was born after the Second World War in 1948, but I feel as if I've trekked across India and fought alongside the courageous Gurkas in Burma: *'The Japs soon shifted themselves when those Gurka boys pulled out their khukuris'. Did I tell you about the rope bridge across this raging river that I crossed driving a ten ton truck? The lads got a fright when I pulled the pin out of a hand grenade by mistake and it dropped on the floor!*

Thanks dad. And you definitely earned that Burma Star ten times over.

I hope you are sitting there now, extending my list with your own instinctive thoughts on a Time Machine journey back to your old house and your old street.

I also hope this second 'Lost Tribe' book has stirred your emotions and encouraged you to sit down for a moment, shut your eyes, think of someone special from your past, and remember a time and place that really was another world, viewed in flickering tones of black and white.

And so I leave you where I brought you in . . .

The journey home is now complete
The Lost Tribe – back in Everton's streets
In our mind's eye, our Nins, our Nans
Our Dads, old Pop, our dear old Grans

Grandad's medals shine again
Reminding us when men were men
Our mams still there to stir our souls
And help us all to reach our goals

The Council sent us far away
They called it our Slum Clearance Day
They built us flats ten storeys high
With 'streets' that floated in the sky

They said we wouldn't have it hard
But High Rise flats don't have a yard
And how are mams supposed to dream
Without a sandstone step to clean?

Why bother with an open door
When Mary's on another floor?
Or even in another town
Why did they knock our old streets down?

But now we've started coming home
To climb Mount Everton and roam
Atop that hill that's still a jewel
The greatest view in Liverpool

THE LOST TRIBE
BACK IN EVERTON'S STREETS . . .

LOST TRIBE

THE PEOPLE'S MEMORIES

WWW.LOSTTRIBEOFEVERTON.COM